Life In His Presence
A Journey into the Supernatural

Sebastián Angulo Negrón

Life In His Presence: A Journey into the Supernatural
Copyright © Sebastian Angulo Negron 2016
Fredericksburg, VA
All rights reserved.
Scripture taken from the New King James Version. Copyright © 1982 by Thomas Nelson, Inc. Used by permission. All rights reserved.
Edited by Sandy Anders
Cover Design by Sebastian Angulo Negron
Original cover photo taken from www.unsplash.com
ISBN   978-0692694299
         0692694293

Dedication

This book is dedicated to my loving family who has been such a powerful force in my life. The encouragement and support that I have received from each has pushed me to where I am today. My father's hunger for God and my mother's dedication to prayer impacted me from a young age. The encounters that my siblings had and that I shared with them in church services, as well as the friendship and company that I shared with them have all served to shape who I am today.

To my dad and prayer partner, Miguel, who taught me integrity from a young age and to hunger for God, who encouraged me continually to follow the Lord's leading in my life.

To my mom, Sylvia, who taught me to respect others and to simply enjoy life, and who took me along with her to the church to pray in the mornings at a young age, an experience I know has had an impact to this day.

To my oldest brother, Gabriel, whose early experiences with God, when he shared them with the family, have made a powerful impact in my life.

To my sister, Raquel, whose ability to listen and give advice has blessed me many times, who has blessed me with a lifetime of hair cuts, and with whom I have laughed often.

To my brother, Daniel, who has been a lifelong friend to me. He has been there with me and for me through most of the vital stages and events of my life. Whose friendship and support have been anchors to me.

Acknowledgements

First of all I would like to thank You Jesus for giving me life and the privilege of knowing You! For blessing me with the opportunity to write this book and giving me all I needed for this project.

I would like to thank Sandy Anders who worked diligently to edit this book on top of all the other projects of her own. I would not have been able to publish this book if it was not for her gracious help. Sandy, the Lord will not *"forget your labor of love which you have shown towards His name, in that you have ministered to the saints and do minister"* (Hebrews 6:10). Thank you Sandy!

I would also like to acknowledge and thank the community at the Fredericksburg Prayer Furnace (FPF) as well as the leadership there that have provided a place I call home. At FPF I have been able to grow and mature in my walk with the Lord and it was in its prayer room that I wrote this book.

Lastly I would like to thank all who have supported me spiritually -- in prayer and encouragement -- and financially over the years for different missions trips, projects (including this one) and for me to be enabled to be in full-time ministry.

Table of Contents

Preface   1

1. The Father's Ways   3
2. Pathway to Glory   27
3. Carrying the Glory   53
4. The Ark of the Covenant   81
5. Hunger: A Key to the Glory   99
6. The Glory of Intercession: Seated in Heavenly Places   131
7. Experiencing the Living Word   155
8. The Way Everlasting   177

Appendix: Biblical References   204

Preface

Every journey has a starting point. Before we launch into this adventure I want to take the opportunity to share with you a little about the nature of the journey we will be taking through the next eight chapters.

I begin this book with a chapter about the Father and His ways. Jesus is the starting point for our journey towards the Father! Jesus said to His disciples, *"I am the way the truth and the life, no one comes to the Father but through me"* (John 14:6). Moses prayed to God *"...Show me now Your way that I may know You..."* (Exodus 33:13). Jesus came to reveal God's way to humanity by His life, death, and resurrection. He was and continues to be the door by which we enter in.

I am glad that you have chosen to read this book and I want to invite you to join me in the adventure. To start on the journey we must go through the door (John 10:9-10). This is a spiritual expedition that cannot be taken without Jesus. If you have never surrendered your life to Jesus, if you cannot say that

Life In His Presence

you know this Man, I invite you to begin a dialogue with Him, seek Him and you will not be disappointed.

The Bible teaches that when we call upon the Name of the Lord we will be saved; from future judgment, from a purposeless life, from the sad reality of not knowing our Loving Creator. Call to Him! Read this prayer, and say it to the Lord if you would like to surrender your life to the Lord, Jesus!

> Jesus, I believe in you, I acknowledge that I need You. I believe that You died on the cross for my sins and that after three days You rose from the dead. I repent of my sins (mention to Him the specific sins you are turning from) and I give you my life. I will serve you for the rest of my life. I am Yours!

You can come back to this prayer at any point during your reading if you feel you are not ready to make such a commitment yet. I pray that as you read this book, whether you have known the Lord for many years or are just now getting acquainted with Him, that you will experience the surpassing greatness of knowing Christ Jesus! That this book will serve as a step in your journey.

Chapter 1

The Father's Ways

A person's ways are a constant—something that does not change, that determines how he will act. If a person is quick-tempered, it is not surprising when he suddenly flares in anger at a small thing. Those who have lived with a group of people for more than a couple of weeks will be able to tell who doesn't flush the toilet, who makes their bed, whose clothes are always lying around on the floor, who clears the dishwasher, etc., because they get to know one another's ways. If someone is gentle-hearted, it is not surprising if he goes out of his way to help someone that fell down, because others know they are gentle-hearted. As we get to know others, we begin to know their ways, or, as we see other's ways, we get to know them. Ways are a constant that can be expected from a person in day-to-day circumstances.

Moses asked God to reveal His ways to him and this, too, is what we must do. *"Oh the depth of the riches both of the wisdom and knowledge of God! How unsearchable are His*

Life In His Presence

judgments and His ways past finding out!" (Romans 11:33). Holy Spirit is the One that searches the deep things of God, His unsearchable ways, and He declares them to us (1 Corinthians 2:9-10; John 16:14). Through what He says about Himself, His glory-filled interactions with His people Israel, and our own encounters with Him, the Holy Spirit will begin to teach us His unsearchable ways.

"Every good and perfect gift is from above and comes down from the Father of lights, with whom there is no variation or shadow of turning" (James 1:17). The Father's ways are always the same. He does not change or shift as the shadows. In the midst of darkness, He still is light, and darkness flees. In the midst of trouble, He is a very present help; He is our refuge (Psalm 46:1). His ways are constant, no matter what the circumstances are. God said to Moses, *"I AM that I AM"* (Exodus 3:14). *"Jesus Christ is the same yesterday, today, and forever"* (Hebrews 13:8). He is constant. He is always good!

The LORD reveals His ways through His actions, through His glory. In Numbers 14:11 the LORD asked Moses, *"How long will they not believe Me, with all the signs which I have performed among them?"* The LORD was revealing Himself to them through signs and wonders. Moses prayed, *"If I have found grace in Your sight, show me now Your way, that I may know You..."* He continued to ask, *"Please show me Your glory (kabod)"* (Exodus 33). The glory brings revelation of His

The Father's Ways   *Chapter 1*

ways.

Moses asked the LORD to show him His ways, and the LORD said, *"I will make all My goodness pass before you..."* The Father's ways overflow from His goodness and from His love. He continued, *"and I will proclaim the name of the LORD before you. I will be gracious to whom I will be gracious, and I will have compassion on whom I will have compassion"* (Exodus 33:19). When the LORD proclaimed His name to Moses, He declared to Moses the essence of who He Is, "I AM," His name. Everything He does overflows from those realities.

"Now the LORD descended in the cloud and stood with him there, and proclaimed the name of the LORD. And the LORD passed before him and proclaimed, 'The LORD, the LORD God, merciful and gracious, longsuffering, and abounding in goodness and truth, keeping mercy for thousands, forgiving the iniquity and transgression and sin, by no means clearing the guilty, visiting the iniquity of the fathers upon the children and the children's children to the third and the fourth generation.' So Moses made haste and bowed his head toward the earth, and worshipped."

                                                                            Exodus 34:5-8

Life In His Presence

Everything He does displays His attributes, whether He is refreshing a person or disciplining a nation. When somebody is very confident, it is visible in His actions and in the way He walks. To one who does not know a person's ways, confidence may be confused with arrogance. In like manner, God's mercy, grace, patience, goodness, and truth can seem harsh or foolish to those who don't know His ways.

Judgments are a very real manifestation of His glory. When the LORD proclaimed His name to Moses, He proclaimed both His goodness and His severity (Romans 11:22). His goodness: *"Keeping mercy for thousands, forgiving iniquity and transgression and sin"* (Exodus 34:7a). His severity: *"by no means clearing the guilty, visiting the iniquity of the fathers upon the children and the children's children to the third and the fourth generations"* (Exodus 34:7b). His ways are like a whirlwind. They do not contradict one another but flow together as one. He has His way in the whirlwind (Nahum 1:3).

We must understand that His severity is not contrary to His name but is an important part of His goodness. A loving God would destroy those things that hinder love, and the LORD will do so. Sin and all that comes along with it must be judged, as must those who will not turn from their wicked ways. A loving God will not bring vessels full of hatred and evil into a place where He will give rest to those who love Him.

The Father's Ways   *Chapter 1*

The Fear of the LORD: Knowing His Ways

There are two aspects of the fear of the LORD on which I would like to touch. One is quite a paradigm shift from the manner in which we normally think of fear. It is a side of the fear of the LORD that is full of trust and displays the foundation of love on which the righteous fear of the LORD is founded. The other aspect is the more common perception we have when we think of the fear of the LORD--that is, the terrifying encounter we have whenever God meets us to reveal Himself. The first is a permanent product of the second when the second--that is the terrifying aspect--is received with humility and submission. This is an important thing to understand, as we will be unable to rightly respond to the revelation of His ways—who He is—apart from the fear of the Lord.

The way the Father teaches us the fear of the LORD is very interesting. He teaches us how to fear Him as a father teaches his son (Deuteronomy 8:5-6). In other words, He teaches us how to respect Him as a father teaches his son to respect him. Most of the interaction between a father and his son should teach the son that his father is kind, fun, adventurous, strong, honest, constant, firm, and more. These interactions teach a son not to be afraid of his father, but to fear his father. God does not teach us as a master teaches a slave, but as a father teaches a son. A son respects his father and trusts him, learning from a young age that with his father there is provision and without his father he would be unable to survive. After all these interactions, a son should begin to know his father's ways, and neither chastising nor enjoyment should come as a surprise.

The means that the LORD used to teach Israel to fear Him are described in verses 3-6 of Deuteronomy 8. He allowed them to hunger, that He might feed them with manna. Their garments did not wear out nor did their feet swell, that they might know His ways and fear Him. However, they did not fear Him rightly; they were afraid He would kill them, and they did not trust that He would do what He had said He would do. Though He was consistent with them, they always expected Him to somehow change. They saw His power, but they did not know His name. They did not know the extent of His power— that He could completely deliver them.

In the desert the Israelites thought God was quick to anger, impatient, unkind, without mercy, and lacking in goodness and truth. They thought He would clear the guilty and not visit the iniquity of the fathers on the children. They did not know His ways, and so they went astray in their hearts. They did not understand His acts as acts of love. They had wrong ideas about Him and completely misinterpreted the purpose for which he was leading them by the hand out of the land of Egypt (Jeremiah 31:32).

The Father's Ways   *Chapter 1*

If you see His acts but don't acquaint them with His ways, then you will only have fear, and not the fear of the Lord. Many are afraid of His ability (power), but do not fear His nature. This is why the Israelites trembled at the bottom of the mountain but still did not turn from their ways.

Awe and trembling in His manifest majesty is the experience we normally think of when we think about the fear of the Lord. In order to know the Father, we must come to terms with His majesty and His glory. It is through the glory that God reveals His nature and His character. He does not separate His power from His character; rather, He reveals one through the other.

"The fear of the LORD is the beginning of knowledge..." (Proverbs 1:7). Does a man fear that which he believes has no power over him? It is therefore in the manifestation of His glory and power that knowledge begins, that we receive understanding. He has power over us. When we realize that He created all things because He wanted to lavish His love on us, then we begin to know His ways. We had nothing to offer to Him, yet He loved us and made us. We were created to be dependent on Him, to fear and to love Him.

He said to Moses, *"I am the LORD. I appeared to Abraham, to Isaac, and to Jacob, as God Almighty, by My name Lord I was not known to them"* (Exodus 6:2-3). Abraham, Isaac, and Jacob did not know the Lord's name, nor did Israel in

Life In His Presence

Moses' days. So He told Moses, *"Therefore say to the children of Israel: 'I am the LORD; I will bring you out from under the burdens of the Egyptians, I will rescue you from their bondage, and I will redeem you with an outstretched arm and with great judgments. I will take you as My people, and I will be your God.* <u>*Then you shall know that I am the LORD your God who brings you out from under the burdens of the Egyptians*</u>. *And I will bring you into the land which I swore to give to Abraham, Isaac, and Jacob; and I will give it to you as a heritage: I am the LORD'"* (Exodus 6:6-7).

Because the children of Israel did not know Him, God told Moses that He would reveal Himself to them as Redeemer, with an outstretched arm and with great judgments. He would reveal Himself to His people as the Lord, mighty to save, and would work in such a way that they would have to trust Him and depend on Him for provision. Yet they did not enter into a Godly fear and dependency on the Lord that would have begun their knowledge of His ways. He led them out of Egypt with an outstretched arm and great judgments, as a Father would lead them by the hand; but they did not continue in His commandments (Hebrews 8:9).

God was dealing with a people that did not know Him, and in His wisdom He chose to reveal Himself to them through His power. He still likes to reveal Himself through His power. He did so to the Corinthians while Paul preached Christ and

Him crucified, not with persuasive words of human wisdom but by preaching the cross (1 Corinthians 2), which is the wisdom and power of God (1 Corinthians 1:24).

I believe that our Christian experience is greatly limited by the lack of fear of the LORD in which we walk. If we want to experience the glory, we need to take hold of the fear of the LORD. God desires to manifest His glory so we will delight in and tremble at His majesty, not so we will have to partake of His wrath when we become offended at His revealing. The glory is available to us today, but I believe it is withheld from us by the mercy of God lest, in our sins and compromise, we perish like Ananias and Sapphira.

The manifest glory of God would destroy most of the foundations upon which believers in the West have built. The effects of His glory would be so detrimental to what we call normal and good that He has given us time to repent, turn, and seek Him. But He will come to us: *"For yet a little while He who is coming will come and will not tarry"* (Hebrews 10:37). When He comes, *HE* comes, not just the parts of Him we like. Isaiah 64 says that the mountains shake when He comes. Our own kingdoms will shake and crumble.

The terrifying presence that covered the mountain and filled the Holiest of All has not changed. It is still the same presence today. In the times of Moses, there was great fear associated with the presence of God; there were notable

Life In His Presence

consequences for opposing His anointed or disobeying His Word. Those who rebelled received severe punishments from the Lord: thousands died, Miriam became leprous for seven days, etc. Many think that things have changed, but the presence of the LORD back then is the same presence today. He has not changed.

His presence is the same. We are the ones that have been changed by the blood of Christ; therefore, we now have greater access to the glory, and it is even within us. Nevertheless, this presence that shook the mountains will once more shake not only the earth, but also the heavens (Hebrews 12). Many do not feel the need for the fear of the LORD as they think Israel must have needed it then, but we need it even more so today. If you question this, read Hebrews 12.

Fear: Not Knowing His Ways

The Israelites in the wilderness did not turn their hearts toward the LORD in Godly fear, even though He had delivered them with a mighty hand and an outstretched arm. Therefore, they did not know the Father's ways. They had bipolar emotions towards the LORD: one moment they were excited that He had heard their cries and would free them; the next moment they thought He was messing with them and trying to make things more difficult for them (Exodus 5:21; 6:9). They saw the glory of God as a cloud by day and a fire by night, leading and preserving them. Yet when Pharaoh's army came after them as they were at the edge of the Red Sea, they complained against God, questioning His motives for leading them out of Egypt and questioning His ability to save them (Exodus 14:11-12). When they came to the Wilderness of Sin, they again complained against God, questioning whether He wanted to starve them to death--even saying that they would rather go back to the bondage from which God had just delivered them (Exodus 16:3).

There were many other times in which they doubted God, including the time they made the golden calf--a great offense. When Moses delayed on the mountain, the people of Israel, not knowing what had become of him, asked Aaron to make gods for them to worship. Though they had seen the many wonders of God and were making covenant with Him, they quickly turned from Him (Exodus 32:1-10). They were obviously questioning the surety of the Word of God, Who is faithful. Faith in God is knowing and trusting that God is both able and faithful to do what He has said He would do. Faith is not true faith without Godly fear, and Godly fear is not the fear of the Lord without faith. He told them not to keep manna overnight but they did, waking up to find worms in it and making the whole camp stink (Exodus 16:20). He also told them that on the morning of the seventh day there would be no manna on the ground, yet they went out looking for it (Exodus

Life In His Presence

16:24-30). They thought that He was changing constantly, instead of remaining constant. They did not know His ways, and so they rebelled. They did not know Him as faithful. He had said it would not appear, and they still searched for it. They did not believe Him. There was unbelief in their hearts.

Over and over again, they questioned the LORD's ability to preserve them and to provide for them. He did many signs and many wonders that they might know Him, trust Him, and know His ways. However, when hardship came, they thought evil of Him--that He meant to harm them. They did not know Him well. They never came to know, as Moses came to know, that God is good and His mercy endures forever.

He did not lay the full revelation of Himself on them all at once, but He still desired them to fear and respect Him with the revelation they had received. He was teaching them His ways through an outstretched arm and great judgments. At first, even Moses had his doubts; but as God revealed Himself, Moses' confidence in His ways increased. He knew he could go up the quaking mountain; he knew he could intercede for the people in the midst of plagues; he knew he could ask Him to go with them; he knew he could ask to see His glory; and he knew that the LORD would listen to him and act on his behalf.

Those who don't know the Father's ways are those who harden their hearts when the Holy Spirit speaks to them. When the Holy Spirit of adoption says, "You are a son," the individual says, "No, I'm an orphan. I'm all alone." When He says, "You are accepted in the Beloved," the individual says, "I will never be good enough." When He says, "I will provide," the individual believes more in his own poverty than in God's provision.

There are those who are so set on their own ways that they will not embrace the ways of the Father. *"Do not be wise in your own eyes; fear the LORD and depart from evil"* (Proverbs 3:7). They participate in a "Christianity" that is *"double-minded, and unstable in all its ways"* (James 1:8). They have not taken off the former chains of slavery to fear, even though freedom has been purchased (Romans 8:15). They do what they do not want to do and have no power to do what they desire to do--still slaves of iniquity, instead of slaves of the righteousness of God (Romans 6:18; 7:14). They would say, *"O wretched man that I am!"* (Romans 7:24); they do not walk according to the Spirit but according to the flesh (Romans 8:1).

These continue to walk according to the course of this world. They do not assume their position as those having been raised with Christ (Ephesians 2:1-6). They have confessed with their mouths but have not believed with their hearts (Romans 10:9).

"Beware brethren, lest there be in any of you an evil heart of unbelief in departing from the living God; but exhort one

Life In His Presence

another daily, while it is still called 'Today,' lest any of you be hardened through the deceitfulness of sin."

Hebrews 3:12-13

"For indeed the gospel was preached to us as well as to them; but the word which they heard did not profit them, not being mixed with faith in those who heard it."

Hebrews 4:2

The main issue here is unbelief. Hebrews chapters 3 and 4 equate unbelief with disobedience. Faith is an expectation when the Uncreated speaks. Those who are in unbelief cannot know His ways and cannot enter into His rest. *"And to whom did He swear that they would not enter His rest, but to those who did not obey: so we see that they could not enter in because of unbelief"* (Hebrews 3:18-19). Faith and confidence in His ways--in His love--produces obedience to His commands. Jesus said, *"If you love Me, you will obey my commandments"* (John 14:15). Love for God necessitates that we confidently receive love from God, for *"We love Him because He first loved us"* (1 John 4:19).

Responding to the Manifestation of His Ways

At the bottom of the mountain, where the Israelites trembled, there was an invitation for them to seek the LORD, to draw near to Him. Every demonstration of His power is an invitation to know Him at a deeper level. It is not simply enough to be present when God manifests His power--a response is required. The fear of the LORD is not just an emotion, but a decision to submit to His ways.

The Israelites were present during most of these demonstrations, yet they did not know Him; they did not accept the invitation to know Him. In a sense, they were satisfied with being distant from Him. In their actions, they displayed the question, "Why seek something you don't need?"

Seeking the LORD is an act of humility. It is an acknowledgment that God has what we need. God does not simply want us to turn from our own ways, but He wants us to turn to Him. In fact, it will be impossible for us to really turn from our wicked ways unless we first turn to Him. We are to turn to Him and seek Him with greater devotion than we had for those things we are turning from. Repentance is not a passive state in which we don't do wrong, but a living and active reality that hungers, seeks, and thirsts for righteousness (Matthew 5:6 and 6:33).

There are qualities of an individual's character that we cannot know unless we search out the individual. As we are around someone we are getting to know, we inquire of them and view their behavior. Whenever they do something unique, we turn to see, we pay attention, and we take note in our hearts.

Life In His Presence

By these means, we come to know a person's ways. It is because He has searched us that the Lord comprehends our paths and is acquainted with all our ways (Psalm 139:1, 3, 23-24). It is the same with the LORD; we have to search Him out to know His ways. *"Seek the LORD while He may be found, call upon Him while He is near. Let the wicked forsake his way, and the unrighteous man his thoughts; let him return to the LORD, and He will have mercy on him; and to our God, for He will abundantly pardon. 'For My thoughts are not your thoughts, nor are your ways My ways,' says the LORD"* (Isaiah 55:6-8).

The right way to respond to God speaking to us is to humble ourselves and to learn, to listen, and to ask questions. What did David like to do in the house of the LORD, the place where His glory dwelt? He desired to behold the beauty of the Lord and to inquire in His temple (Psalm 26:8; 27:4).

Moses' Response

Moses began seeking the Lord early on. His response to God's demonstrations was to seek Him. When God would demonstrate, Moses would turn from his way to acknowledge the LORD. He would then inquire of the LORD, and more understanding would be given to him. Then, as more was given, He again would inquire of the LORD.

The Father's Ways   Chapter 1

    When Moses first encountered the LORD, he turned to see the bush that was aflame but not being consumed. He did not know God or His ways. Therefore, he doubted the LORD's ability to do through him what He said He would do. He did not just question once or twice, but many times even after that first encounter with God:

1. Moses said, "Who am I that I should go to Pharaoh?" He was basically asking, "Are you sure you got the right guy? Can you even use me?" (Exodus 3:11)
2. He questioned the omniscient One, saying, "What if they don't believe me? What if what You are saying does not happen, and they don't believe?" (Exodus 4:1). In response, God promised signs and wonders.
3. Moses, though in the presence of God who would deliver the people of Israel out of Egypt, feared a snake. (Exodus 4:3)
4. Moses deemed himself, whom God had qualified, unqualified, because his speech was not eloquent. He did not realize that God was not interested in what Moses had to offer, but in his willingness. God did not want persuasive words of human wisdom, but demonstrations of power. (Exodus 4:10)
5. Moses insisted that he was unqualified, resisting the wisdom of God, and God's anger was kindled against Moses.

19

Life In His Presence

(Exodus 4:13-14)

6. Moses said to God, "Why is it You have sent me to Pharaoh...he has done evil to Your people and You have not delivered them?" (Exodus 5:22-23)
7. Moses questioned God's sending him to Pharaoh, saying, "If Israel did not heed me, why should Pharaoh?" He was really asking, "Are You able to do what you said, and will You ensure Pharaoh moves in response to Your word, when Your own people won't?" (Exodus 6:12)

This questioning happened many times--possibly more times than what I've shared. At those points of questioning, Moses did not know God's ways, and therefore he doubted the LORD. God had just started talking to Moses, and he was still getting to know Him. He was about to find out that the LORD had all power and did what He said He would do. As Moses saw God's works, he began to humble himself before the LORD and to trust Him. He realized that God was God and deserving of glory, honor, blessing, and trust.

The LORD showed Moses His glory, *"So Moses made haste and bowed his head toward the earth, and worshipped"* (Exodus 34:8). There is a right way to respond to the glory of God, and there is a wrong way. How one responds to the glory determines what one receives from the glory. Moses learned to choose the better way, which is the fear of the Lord. The difference between Moses and the rest of the Israelites is that he humbled himself before the LORD. As he humbled himself before the LORD, Moses received revelation knowledge and was spoken to by God as a friend. Israel, however, did not humble themselves before the LORD. As a result of their arrogant response to the glory, they received judgments and a hardened heart. Moses was able to acquaint himself with the LORD, who acted on Israel's behalf; the rest of the Israelites were not. He was not called stiff-necked as they were. God's ways are displayed in the glory but are not received apart from humility. Whoever does not humble himself in the glory of God cannot receive the revelation of His ways.

A New and Living Way

"*But what are we that you complain against us?*" (Exodus 16:7b). This is what Moses and Aaron said to the people when they came to them complaining about their circumstances. Moses and Aaron were basically saying, "What authority do we have in ourselves that you so complain against us? We don't have what you need." Israel's confidence was in human ability, not God's. Therefore, they were easily shaken when they faced situations they could not control. The Lord wanted the children of Israel to come before Him confident of His provision, not in complaint over their lack. Moses told Aaron to say to all the children of Israel *"Come near before the*

Life In His Presence

Lord, for He has heard..." (Exodus 16:9b). He is the God who hears and who acts. God wanted them to come to Him, but they turned to men. God wanted them to trust in His provision, but they feared their lack. However, He always provided. The LORD is the source. He is Father.

We have not done anything to deserve God's love or His help. He had chosen Israel to be His people, and even they struggled to trust Him. If they who had His favor were not confident in Him, what assurance do we have? In Christ, not only does God adopt us as sons, but He cleanses us from our sins, and He sees Jesus every time He looks at us. Christ became the surety of a better covenant (Hebrews 7:22). Our confidence is that not only is He good, but He has clothed us with His goodness! God is willing and able to complete His promises to us. If it were up to us, we would have nothing in which to be confident. We could only hope that our past would be forgotten and that we wouldn't get caught the next time we messed up. Our confidence would have to be on our ability to get a job and make enough money to provide for ourselves and family. We don't have to put our hope in our own strength but can simply lean on Him. We can be confident that when we humble ourselves before God we will receive His grace and will be exalted by Him.

The Israelites in the wilderness experienced the glory, and many times their response caused them great suffering. I believe that that glory is the same glory we want today. We can put our confidence in the blood of Jesus rather than in our own righteousness and know that we can have "boldness to enter the Holiest" (Hebrews 10:19).

His ways are *unto* something. They lead somewhere. His ways lead us into His rest--that is, into confidence in His finished work. It was because they--those in the wilderness--went astray in their hearts and did not know His ways that He swore, "They shall not enter My rest" (Psalm 95).

Moses cried out to God, that He would show him His way. Jesus said *"I am the way, the truth, and the life…"* (John 14:6). Essentially, when Moses asked the LORD to show him His Way, whether he realized it or not, he was asking God to show him His Son. He was asking to see *"the brightness of His glory--the express image of His Person"* (Hebrews 1:3). Jesus is the Way, and He perfectly portrays the ways of the Father.

Philip said to Jesus, *"Lord, show us the Father, and it is sufficient for us."* Jesus responded to Philip, *"He who has seen Me has seen the Father…"* (John 14:8-9B). Philip requested the same thing that Moses had requested thousands of years before, yet he was unaware that the fulfillment of his request was present and already granted to him.

In Jesus is the complete manifestation of the glory of God. Everything that He does portrays the person of God; every work He did displayed the Father's ways. Our confidence is that

Life In His Presence

the One who is the way to the Father has given us access through the veil of His flesh. *"Therefore, brethren, having boldness to enter the Holiest by the blood of Jesus, by a new and living way which He consecrated for us, through the veil, that is, His flesh, and having a High Priest over the house of God, let us draw near with a true heart in full assurance of faith, having our hearts sprinkled from an evil conscience and our bodies washed with pure water..."* (Hebrews 10:19-22).

The way is through the finished work of Christ on the cross. Because it is finished, we already know the results and can appropriate the recompense of that for which He labored. No longer do we have to strive for that which we don't have access to, but now we can simply step into it. *"For he who has entered His rest has himself also ceased from his works as God did from His"* (Hebrews 4:10).

When we know His ways, we can be confident to ask Him for things we need rather than to complain against Him and turn to men, as the children of Israel did in the desert. Orphans beg and complain. Sons approach the throne and ASK (Ask, Seek, and Knock) with boldness and confidence that God, being a great Father, will give the Holy Spirit to those who ask Him (Luke 11:10-13). Jesus said that we could ask the Father anything in His name and the Father would give it to us.

The Israelites in the desert witnessed many of His acts but did not get acquainted with the God who acted on their

The Father's Ways   *Chapter 1*

behalf. They saw His works, but never made a connection between His works and His ways. Therefore, as the scriptures say, *"Today, if you will hear His voice, do not harden your hearts as in the rebellion, in the day of trial in the wilderness, where your fathers tested Me, tried Me, and saw My works forty years"* (Hebrews 3:7-9).

    In the coming chapters, we will explore the ways of the Father and the manifestation of His presence that give us glimpses into who He is and what He is like. We will discover how to enter into that wonderful presence. As we linger there and behold His glory, we will come to know His ways more and we will be transformed into His likeness.

Life In His Presence

Chapter 2

Pathway to Glory

We enter His Gates with Thanksgiving, His Courts with Praise (Psalm 100:4); then we Worship in the Beauty of Holiness (Psalm 29); and as the train of His robe fills the temple (Isaiah 6), we Stand in the Glory/Gaze on the Beauty of the Lord.

There is an actual procession in which we "enter in'" and each part of it will be expounded upon in the following pages. Ruth Heflin writes in her book, *Glory: Experiencing the Atmosphere of Heaven*, "Praise until the spirit of worship comes, worship until the Glory comes, then stand in the Glory." And that is how it happens.

Thanksgiving is exalting God for what He has done, for His Works. It is motivated by the joy that is produced in us for what He has done. There is a time for it and that time is when we are entering His gates. Thanksgiving is an overflow of gratefulness that one experiences as one gets to enter in *"by a new and living way which He consecrated for us, through the veil, that is, His flesh"* (Hebrews 10:20). It is the fruit of our lips. It is what is produced as we approach and enter through the veil, that is, His flesh. It is the overflow of a joy-filled heart because of what has been purchased for us and because our debt was paid for us. When we see the gates and enter in, we cannot help but thank Him for what He has done.

Let's focus on High Praise for a moment, that is, praise that comes from above. Praise, unlike thanksgiving, is not exalting God for what He has done, but for who He is. It is not focused on oneself, as thanksgiving still involves the individual in the topic for which they are grateful. It is the exaltation of His Ways. Once we go through the gates and see His Splendor and Majesty, the natural response is praise. It's an outburst of the ecstasy that is found in beholding Him.

Thanksgiving and praise lead us into the place of adoration, the place of awe, the place of worship. We start out with exuberant joy, making joyful noises unto the Lord… jumping, spinning, dancing in thankfulness… declaring His wonders and shouting. These praises take place in the multitudes. Paraphrasing Ruth Heflin as she describes Jesus' entrance into Jerusalem on a donkey: The crowds shouted Hosanna, and we are shouting with the crowd; but when He is right in front of you on His donkey, you cannot help but bow down before him and pour out love at His feet, to intimately whisper to Him the deep love that you have for Him. Praise is in the assembly, worship is in the chamber (Hebrews 2:12; Song of Songs 1:4).

All of these are expressions of intimacy and cannot be expressed without a level of the knowledge of God. Thanksgiving cannot exist if we don't know what He has done for us. Praise cannot exist if we don't know His Ways. Worship cannot exist if we do not know Love.

These three are heavenly substance and are not produced apart from the Holy Spirit. They are the substance of *"now Faith"* (Hebrews 11:1). They are the substance of a present encounter with God, a reaction to His Beauty. Isaiah 57:19 says that God creates the fruit of our lips and Hebrews 13:15 says that praise and thanksgiving are the fruit of our lips. There really is a difference, as Ruth would say, between created praise and just normal words coming out of our mouths. Though we don't have to worry about it being real or not, we just need to do it in faith.

God is not interested in the praises of man, praises that man has to offer, but He is interested in the praises of God. The rich man came to Jesus saying "good teacher" and Jesus responded saying, "Why do you call me good?" The praises of man are founded on man's knowledge; the praises of God are founded upon the knowledge of God. They actually are God's praises that He places in us. *"Let the high praises of God be in*

Life In His Presence

their mouths and a two-edged sword in their hands" (Psalms 149:6). They are not the praises <u>for</u> God, but the praises <u>of</u> God--they belong to Him, and they come from Him. Just like the two-edged sword in their hands is the Word of God, the high praises in their mouths are the praises of God. He is interested in that which can only be accessed by faith, in that which comes from the place of revelation.

Common Roadblocks to the Pathway

Being led by Feelings

The procession into His presence is not a feeling reality but a faith reality. Many people feel hindered in their ability to praise God, or worship Him, because they "cannot feel it." All that this path requires is the knowledge of God, and you cannot possibly be saved without having a level of the knowledge of God.

If you know that He is Good, then you have reason to thank Him, you have reason to praise Him, you have access to worship Him. If you believe that He created the heavens and the earth, that He was hung on a tree for our sins, that He was resurrected on the third day, and that He ever lives to make intercession for us, then you have what you need to worship Him. If you believe that He is Good but cannot write a paper on it or preach it, you can still praise Him. There is no excuse, there is no limit, there is no boundary--we can choose to believe Him and Praise Him or we can choose to doubt Him.

Did Jesus say that God is Spirit and that those who worship Him will worship Him in <u>soul</u> and in <u>feelings</u>? Did He say that one has to feel it or else it's not genuine? Or even that, if we don't feel it, we don't have to praise Him? NO! He said, *"God is Spirit, and those who worship Him will worship Him in Spirit and in Truth"* (John 4:24). Regardless of how tired, lazy, guilty, disconnected, shameful, depressed, angry, happy, distracted, sinful, lustful, sad, unbelieving, etc., we feel, He is Worthy to be praised!

We access the Spirit and Truth dimension of worship through faith. Spirit: We are already there to behold Him by the Spirit of Christ. Truth: We are accepted in the beloved, we are sons of God, we place our confidence on the finished work of Christ, that He is Good and that He is always the same. We don't praise Him because we feel like it, we do so because He is Worthy!

Lack of Faith and Perseverance

He says in Hebrews 11:6, *"Without faith it is impossible to please Him, for those who come to God must believe that He is and that He is a rewarder of those who diligently seek him."* He is pleased with those who come before Him with expectation, regardless of how they feel, believing that God Is,

Life In His Presence

and that He is a rewarder of those who diligently seek Him.

Often people begin to praise or pray in the spirit but find it is hard to do so. There seems to be a bit of a wall or a hindrance. In those times we just need to press through, or to praise through. When you praise through, you are tilling the ground and preparing the environment for the presence of the King. So when you don't feel it, just do it anyways. Do it with force, do it with faith, and pay attention to see as the atmosphere in your heart and the atmosphere around you shifts.

Sometimes we just have to wake ourselves up and come out of agreement with dullness and apathy. We must purpose in our hearts that we are going to encounter God and not letting go until we do. In other words, whether or not you feel like declaring His wonders, you decide to do so and to do so with "oomph"!

Sin

Sin is definitely a block in this pathway, for God is light and in Him there is no darkness at all. Any unconfessed sins that have not been repented of and are thereby not covered by the blood are roadblocks. Here are just a few:

1. Apathy – Isaiah 64:4,7

2. Impurity – Matthew 5:8; Hebrews 12:14

3. Unbelief – Hebrews 3:19; 11:6

4. Earthly pleasures, desire for riches, and cares – Luke 21:34

5. Disunity – Matthew 18:20
6. Shame – Hebrews 4:16

Entertainment & Distractions

Not all things that will keep us from seeking God are sinful. Some are legitimate pleasures that become distractions and keep us satisfied without His presence. The greatest hindrance to the enjoyment of a seven-course meal may not be a poison that kills a person but rather a bag of chips that fills him prior to the meal. If we fill ourselves with media and entertainment, we may find ourselves already satisfied when we try to read the Bible or pray. The key is not disconnecting from media but it is to purpose ourselves and position our lives by the way that we use our time that He, Jesus, would be our number one pursuit!

Often times, things that are not necessarily sinful keep us from gaining what we would like in God. My dad told me once when I was young that in our search for God "good enough is the enemy of the best." If we are satisfied with what we have, then we will not long for more. God gives a condition to finding Him, and it is wholeheartedness. *"You will seek Me and find Me, when you search for Me with all your heart"* (Jeremiah 29:13).

Life In His Presence

Thanksgiving and Praise

There are many outward expressions of Love for the Lord and of Rejoicing in Him. Thanksgiving and Praise are often in celebration of the Lord's Ways and Attributes and therefore most of the expressions are a celebration of God.

Clapping (Psalm 47:1), Singing, Dancing, Shouting, Rejoicing, Ascribing. When these expressions are done in reaction to the splendor and majesty of God, they are praise unto God and they are praise from God. All of these are important expressions, and I believe the significance of many of these has been overlooked.

I want to focus on ascribing for a moment. The word *yahab* appears several times in the Old Testament meaning to ascribe, to give or to bring God what is due to Him (Psalm. 29:1; 96:7, 1 Chronicles 16:28). Psalm 29:1-2 says, *"Give unto the LORD, O you mighty one, give unto the LORD glory and strength, Give unto the LORD the glory due to His Name, worship the LORD in the beauty of Holiness."* Another word also used in Psalm 29 that means to give, to ascribe, or to thrust, is *nâthan*. In Psalm 68:34 it is used in the same way as verses 1-2 of Psalm 29.

This is a very common expression that we often do without actually engaging in it. To ascribe is to declare to the Lord who He is in exaltation of His greatness, to give Him glory for who He is. It is to thrust praises to Him like, "You are

Holy, Lord," "Worthy is Your Name," "You are Worthy to receive Blessing, Honor, Glory, and Power," "Your Name is Wonderful," "Glory!" etc. These are all examples of ascribing.

Anyone can say "You are holy" but not everyone ascribes "You are Holy!" There is a difference in consciousness of His majesty when you simply say good things about God and when you ascribe wonderful things about the Lord. Any of these listed expressions are empty without faith in the heart of the worshipper.

The word *nâthan* is also used in Psalm 29:11: *"The LORD will give strength to His people; the LORD will bless His people with peace."* Psalm 29 begins with a command that we should ascribe to the LORD glory and strength, and ends saying that the LORD will give us strength. When we ascribe to Him, He will ascribe to us. When we declare His Glory, we will begin to experience it.

One of the main prophets during David's reign was actually named Nathan. I believe this was significant as in that season Israel was ascribing to the LORD glory and strength, the Glory due to His Name. God in response was giving His people Israel strength and peace. Speaking through Nathan, God says to the leader of the nation of Israel, *"I have been with you wherever you have gone, and have cut off all your enemies from before you, and have made you a name like the name of the great men who are on the earth"* (1 Chronicles 17:8).

Life In His Presence

Deuteronomy 6:4-5 says, *"Hear, O Israel: the LORD our God, the LORD is one! You shall Love the LORD your God with all your heart, with all your soul, and with all your strength."* Praise and Thanksgiving require everything that we have to give, not just words from our mouths but from all our heart, soul, and strength.

Thanksgiving and Praise are weapons of warfare; they shift atmospheres and drive back the activity and oppression of the enemy. Psalm 22 says that God sits enthroned on the praises of His people. Praise is so effective as warfare because it ushers in the rule and the dominion of God into any place or situation. *"Where the Spirit of the Lord is there is liberty"* (2 Corinthians 3:16) and *"God is light and in Him there is no darkness"* (1 John 1:5).

When we praise, not only does the dominion of Christ manifest on the earth, but we also ascend into the heavens. We *"enter His gates with thanksgiving and His courts with praise"* (Psalm 100:4). It is not only entering and thereby changing our surroundings, but we ourselves are entering eternal surroundings. We are already seated in heavenly places in Christ; when we praise, we partake of what has been purchased and of the access that has been granted us there.

Praise is a throne for God to sit upon, incense that arises filling the atmosphere. Malachi prophesied, *"From the rising of the sun to its going down, My Name shall be great among the nations and from every place incense will rise..."* (Malachi 1:11). That incense is the high praises of God, where the greatness of His Name is being declared and His fame, the knowledge of His glory, is filling the earth.

This is how you carry the presence: you create a context; you set up a throne, where God can rest and have dominion; and you keep it set up, not tearing it down. The psalmist writes in Psalm 84:4: *"Blessed are those who dwell in Your house; they will still be praising You." Psalm 34:1 tells us, "I will bless the Lord at all times, His praise shall continually be in my mouth."*

High Praise is not something we work up but something that overflows. We access praise by faith and it bubbles up out of us. One of my most significant experiences with praise came about after I had been to a Pentecostal Campground in Ashland, Virginia, and then a couple of months later at Awaken the Dawn 2005. In those places I danced before the Lord and praised His Name more freely, but when I went back to my church I did not worship with that freedom. For weeks and months after these events, I felt a passion stirring up within me but never knew how to express it. It kept building up more and more, but I didn't know how to get it out. I would ask myself during worship services, "Should I scream from the top of my lungs... yell... what should I do?"

Finally one Sunday service I couldn't hold it in any longer, so I took a step forward and began leaping. Although I

Life In His Presence

stepped on a friend's foot, I couldn't stop to apologize, at least not at that point. So I began to dance and jump around screaming Hallelujah from the top of my lungs. In my mind I wondered if everyone thought I was going crazy and hoped that nobody would come and ask me to stop. Although I could have worked up the actions, I could not have worked up these praises. What was being released in the Spirit, the high praises of God, was something that only the Spirit could produce. They were an overflow of the Love of God that had been filling me.

Now this is not to say that it has to feel like this to be the real deal. Remember this is not a "feeling" reality but a "faith" reality. The point of this testimony is to demonstrate the overflow reality of the High Praises of God. Ever since that experience, I understood that I had to follow the Holy Spirit's prompting to praise God with all of my strength!

Worship

The transition from each stepping-stone in the pathway is many times a continuation of the communion that was being experienced but with an increased awareness of who God is. When you move into worship, many times you will say with your mouth the same things that you said while you were in high praise, but in worship you may whisper them while in high praise you were shouting them. It's still the same Person that we are worshipping but the communion moves from the courts into the King's chamber.

Everything we do can and should be as worship unto the Lord. We need that aspect of worship and it is a part of keeping and carrying the presence of God. But that is not what I am talking about right now. I'm talking about a purposed experience where we pour out fragrance at His feet. We actually can and should set aside time to worship Him, really to practice all of these: thanksgiving, praise, and worship.

I wonder how many people have really experienced worship, being in the King's chamber and overcome with Love for the Son of Man. Overcome with a Love that flows out. We actually can experience it.

In the place of worship there is reverence and adoration in response to the Majesty of God. The busyness of American culture and the excitement expected by it do not make much room for this place, worship. It really is a wonderful place, and when you are in that place, you wish you could stay there for the rest of your life, for it is why you were created. It is a place where your focus is solely set on the Lord and on lavishing Love upon Him.

Much of what we call a time of worship is really just a time where there is "worship" music being played. Most of us during this time are distracted though trying to engage with the Lord, thinking about what we should wear the next day, or what we should have said to that person we had debated with earlier

Life In His Presence

that day. But in that time our hearts have not really connected with the Lord and we have not been awed by His Beauty; our hearts haven't overflowed with words full of Love.

We need to actually purpose in our hearts to lavish Love upon Him and many times the procession to that place first begins with thanksgiving, proceeds with praise, and continues into worship.

Mary of Bethany and Mary Magdalene both tapped into this place of worship as they poured out tears and fragrant oil at the Lord's feet. These are some of the most wonderful illustrations of worship in the scriptures, and I'm sure that they never forgot the moment when they bowed before Jesus in full acknowledgement of who He is.

The extravagance of their worship was an overflow of the Love that they had both experienced and partaken of as they encountered the embodiment of Love. Mary of Bethany sat at His feet (Luke 10) and there received an impartation of Love that she proceeded to pour out at His feet. Mary Magdalene too, having encountered Love as He forgave her, loved much and poured out fragrance on Him.

"And behold a woman in the city who was a sinner, when she knew that Jesus sat at the table in the Pharisee's house, brought an alabaster flask of fragrant oil, and stood at His feet behind Him weeping; and she began to wash His feet with her tears,

and wiped them with the hair of her head; and she kissed His feet and anointed them with the fragrant oil... Therefore I say to you, her sins which are many are forgiven, for she loved much. But to whom little is forgiven, the same loves little."

Luke 7:37-38,47

And when Jesus was in Bethany at the house of Simon the leper, a woman came to Him having an alabaster flask of very costly fragrant oil, and she poured it on His head as He sat at the table. But when His disciples saw it, they were indignant, saying, "Why this waste?"...

Matthew 26:6-8

Public displays of affection toward God are often followed by persecution from those around who are unaware of the Majesty of God that causes such extravagance. Worship will often require an abandonment to self that does not regard man's opinion but only God's. A lover's interaction with his beloved is not based on who's around but on the Love that is in them to express.

I want to encourage you, if there are realities that you see in the Bible and you desire them, to meditate on scriptures that talk about that reality. If you desire this intimate Love for Jesus, I encourage you to meditate on Matthew 26 and Luke 7, on the portions that describe the extravagant love expressed

Life In His Presence

there. Faith is the substance of those realities and it comes by hearing and hearing by the Word of God (Hebrews 11:1; Romans 10:17).

We were created to stand in awe of the splendor of His majesty, to see Him and to desire Him ... to see His greatness and shake, yet to be confident and to have the desire to go before Him.

The Hebrew word for worship is *shâchâh* and means to bow down, to fall flat on the ground, to worship. When the raw presence of God was made manifest to individuals in the scriptures, *shâchâh* was many times their response. Most times in the Old Testament when you see the English word worship, the Hebrew word used is *Shâchâh*. I have come to greatly appreciate this word and its meaning. Before I knew what it meant I found myself saying it often when I prayed to the Lord in the spirit. He is completely worthy of our surrender before Him. He is worthy of us laying everything down.

When Moses encountered the Glory of God on the mountain, the Bible says that "he made haste and bowed down." At that point, he did not have much of a choice but had to fall down and worship. When you encounter the Beauty of Holiness, only one response is appropriate and that is to worship. When you hear the voice of God, the Word of God, only one response is appropriate…to tremble.

Carrying the presence of God is a combination of Seeking Him and responding rightly to His Glory when you find Him. Isaiah 66:1-2 says: *"Thus says the LORD: 'Heaven is my throne, and the earth is my footstool; what is the house that you would build for me, and what is the place of my rest? All these things my hand has made, and so all these things came to be,' declares the LORD. But this is the one to whom I will look; he who is humble and contrite in spirit and trembles at my word."*

I long for those encounters with the Lord, the ones where His Glory manifests in such a way that one must *shâchâh*. I do want to encourage you that we do not have to wait for that intensity to fall flat on our faces. Let's continue to long for it and expect it. Daniel, Ezekiel, John the Revelator, and many others had this similar experience when they encountered the Beauty of Holiness.

Often in the scriptures, worship was commanded. Psalm 29:2 tells us to *"worship the Lord in the Beauty of Holiness."* As I mentioned earlier, these are all faith realities, and when we first begin to step into them, we may not feel so much, but things will begin to open up. To worship the LORD was commanded. They were not required to make God appear before them so that they could fall flat on their faces, but they were expected to remember that He is Holy and to respond. With that said, let's pursue the presence of God to the point that

Life In His Presence

we can no longer stand. That is the point of this teaching, to stir desire for the presence of God and to give a grid for the procession into the Glory that God lays out in the scriptures.

Being in the Glory

There is yet a further place to enter into, or to rest in. As I write these notes, I am reminded that thanksgiving, praise, and worship, are intermingled with one another and there are greater depths to each one. We go from glory to Glory and we can always step into a higher praise, a deeper worship, and a greater Glory. "Further up and Further in" as Lewis writes in the *Chronicles of Narnia*.

It is as we behold the Beauty, the Glory of the Lord, that we are transformed and enabled to go on to glory and then to glory and then to…. We cannot exhaust any of these realities. While the glory has been there from the beginning, our awareness of it increases each step of the way. The manifestation of God is greater the deeper we go.

"Lord, I have loved the habitation of Your House, the place where Your Glory dwells."

Psalm 26:8

As we go deeper and deeper, past the gates, past the courts, into the Beauty of Holiness, the Glory--or our awareness of Him--increases. We come to a point where words are too costly and silence alone can express His reality. Where the priests can no longer stand, where nothing we can do can suffice, He has His Way. It is when the presence of God becomes so manifest to the worshipper that words or actions are no longer sufficient, and the worshipper can but gaze into the Beauty in awe.

We experience a little bit of this sometimes in worship services but many of us have yet to be in a meeting where the Glory cloud manifests and we fall flat on our faces. The higher we go in the praises, the deeper our worship and encounter will be. A prime example was the Morningstar conference where they spent hours in High Praise and the cloud was physically manifested, "ruining" everyone who was present as they collapsed onto the floor, wishing they could go even lower than the floor would allow. We enter His gates, then His courts, then His chamber, and finally we are overcome by His presence and just abide in it.

What happens in the Glory? A lot! The worlds were created. People are healed. The invisible becomes visible. The inexistent becomes tangible. Revelation is poured out. There is unity. Heavenly realities and substance manifests. Shadows heal. There is freedom. More. And we are Transformed into His likeness from glory to Glory.

Life In His Presence

From Glory to Glory

There is a difference between the presence of God and the Person of God. When a king enters a city or a palace, his presence is in that city and even more so in that palace, but what about in His Chamber? The city is filled with light because of the King's presence, the city is filled with Glory because of the King's presence, but there is the understanding that there is more and more the closer you get to the King.

There are quantities (for lack of a better word) of the Glory, of the manifest presence of Consuming Fire. There is a level of the Glory, which I believe we have access to, and that God sometimes pours out sovereignly that will save entire cities and even nations. I can think of Wales, Azusa Street, the Jesus Movement, the Great Awakenings, Nineveh at Jonah's preaching, Samaria when Phillip went there, Jesus' ministry, etc.

The point here is that though the Glory cloud may not be physically manifest we may still be accessing the realm of glory. There is more and more, and there are greater measures, but let's be grateful with every level we tap into, and be faithful to glorify Him and to enjoy Him.

In this I do not want to minimize the reality of the Glory, and its potential, for in it the Lord created the heavens and the earth. However, I do want to say that we now have access to His manifest presence and can actually grow in our encounter with His presence. We can go from glory to Glory. You don't have to be able to feel it in your body for it to be the Glory, though sometimes you will. That is not the only way we know if it is the Glory.

"... without faith it is impossible to please God, for he who comes to God must believe that He is and that He is a rewarder of those who diligently seek Him."

Hebrews 11:6

Presently we may not be experiencing the Glory as they may have experienced it in the early church, or as was experienced in the 50's, or as is experienced in other nations or ministries. We presently have access and a means of growing in it as we Worship the Lord in the Beauty of Holiness.

The Lord will pour out His Spirit on all flesh; meanwhile as we await the greater manifestations to come, let's take hold of what is already ours as part of our contending for the greater. Let's not wait for a greater Glory to start worshipping. Let's drink in what has already been freely given to us. Let's be faithful with what we now have and then step into the "more" as He pours it out.

It is righteous to expect greater things from God and even to understand that there is more, but it is unrighteous when, because of this understanding, we get distracted and

Life In His Presence

don't take hold of what He now has for us. If we don't take hold of what is now available to us, what our fathers in the faith have fought for and gained, how will we be prepared to take hold of what is not yet? If we don't climb the steps that they ascended, how will we reach beyond. It is in the wrestling with God and contending for more that the blessing comes and that we are prepared to steward it (Genesis 32:24-30).

There is apathy and complacency that has come over people who desire the move of God. It has come about because they are unrighteous in their waiting, expecting God to do everything for them, rather than partnering with Him in the present. In all of Abraham's waiting he left his family, he gave up his only son, he interceded for Lot, He gave Melchizedek a tenth of the spoils, etc. His waiting was not absent of action, and neither should our waiting be, except for absent of the actions that come from the flesh, from our own strengths.

Unless we by faith take hold of these realities, we will never get to experience the greater things. Had Abraham waited for the promises to come to pass before he started walking to a land he did not know (Hebrews 11), He would never have stepped into the greater things. *"We walk by faith and not by sight."* If I had waited for a major healing anointing before I hit the streets, I would not have seen the number of miracles that I have and probably would not have even known whether the greater had even come. True rest, then, is to be in agreement with the Father, not sitting down and doing nothing. Understand, true waiting on the Lord is an action, gazing is an action, soaking is an action, spreading out our wings and flying is an action (even though the wind is doing the work). Unrighteous waiting is that which does not spread its wings.

I've emphasized greatly our participation with the Lord in entering in and pressing through. I believe that this is an important posture that we must be conscious of lest we fall into a complacent posture. Hebrews teaches that we should strive to enter His rest (Hebrews 4:11). Now I want to emphasize the need to be still. There are so many worries and anxieties that people face, and it is time to simply relax. When you are in the presence of God, it is time to stop doing and to just be. Sometimes it is hard to sit still and not do anything, but there is a great value in enjoying His presence and in being still before Him. The Lord wants to be with us without us having any other agenda but to be with Him.

Positioning Ourselves

Being in the Glory is simply positioning ourselves to receive from the presence of God and to ascend higher and Higher into His presence. A common expression of this reality is what we call "soaking." Soaking, being filled with the Holy Spirit, with the presence of God, more and more, is a part of the procession and greatly impacts your ability to return to that

Life In His Presence

place of encounter. We can spend so much time there that we learn to stay there throughout the day, carrying the presence of the Lord wherever we go. He is all around us; we simply need to be aware of Him in every moment of our day.

Soaking can be an easy practice around people that have learned to cultivate the presence of God. When God's presence is manifest in a tangible way, it is easier to *"Be still and know that He is God"* (Psalm 46). Also, when our heart is already fixed on the Beauty of Jesus through praise and worship, soaking then is simply a continuation. We can certainly tap into the Glory others have already paved a way for; but when there is not a paved road and things are not nicely set up, we can tap into the Glory of Heaven with our Praises paving a way for the Kingdom on earth as it is in Heaven.

As we grow in these realities, we learn more and more how to enter right in, and it is not wrong to do so, though often it is more beneficial to go in little by little. We learn to go right into worship and do not have to spend as long praising; we learn to enter into His presence without having been worshipping as long. Also, as these realities become regular disciplines and delights, it is easier to enter into any of them since we become constantly aware of His presence already around us.

If you find that you are having a hard time soaking, I want to encourage you to enter into soaking from the starting place of thanksgiving, then high praise, then worship, and then into soaking, as opposed to jumping right into soaking. I believe your experience while soaking will be richer when the airs have already been cleared; praise clears the atmosphere. Sometimes you *shâchâh* as soon as you start. The end of all of this is communion with God, and we don't need to rush it or navigate it through our own accord. If you immediately experience a deep worship and begin soaking, go for it.

Lastly, don't be quick to move on. People often finish their time of encounter when they feel the presence of God, instead of resting and waiting on the Lord and enjoying Him, which is the true waiting. It is when you become more aware of His manifest presence that you need to linger. Ruth Heflin compares this to a multiple-course meal versus a fast food restaurant. When you eat at a fast food restaurant, you don't really enjoy the environment--it's a sit-eat-go experience. But we need to push the pause button on the cares of this world, on the desires for riches--actually, we need to lay them down--and then enjoy the time with the Lord just as we would a wonderful multi-course dinner at an exclusive restaurant. Enjoy the time where we minister to Him and He ministers to us, just by being in each other's presence.

Instead of feeling as though we have accomplished something or reached a certain place in procession up the Holy Hill of the Lord and then quitting, we ought to remain there. A

Life In His Presence

good model for this is what the Lord gave the children of Israel in the desert. Wherever the Glory of the Lord rested, there they would pitch their tents and linger, ministering to the Lord for however long the Glory remained in their midst (Numbers 9).

A Corporate Reality

This reality of entering into the Glory of the Lord, of abiding and remaining in it is both a corporate and individual reality. Individuals are able to enter it and carry it just as well as groups of people. God wants both, and ultimately it will culminate with the *"Spirit and the Bride"* saying *"Come."* At that time Jesus will return to the planet and finally the Father Himself will set up His throne in the Heavenly City.

Individuals that live a life of praise can go right into the different steps on the Pathway of Glory pretty easily. But often times in corporate settings, which I believe is the main setting this was designed for, each step is necessary. And we all have to go in together. David talks about this in the Psalms and specifically in Psalm 42:4 where he leads a multitude into the house of God. *"...I used to go with the multitude; I went with them to the house of God, with the voice of joy and praise, with a multitude that kept a pilgrim feast."* This is a corporate reality and we must go in together. Every individual in a corporate setting adds to or takes from the momentum of the procession into the presence of God.

Chapter 3

Carrying the Glory

Glory is the very essence that destroys all in opposition to it. It killed an Israelite who touched it irreverently, and it went before the children of Israel in battle against their enemies to destroy them. This is the Glory that has been made readily available for us to enter into and even carry with us.

We carry this treasure in earthen vessels (2 Corinthians 4:7). Christ in us is the hope of Glory (Colossians 1:27). It is the very strength and might of the Holy Spirit that allows for such an incredible reality. Paul prayed that, *"according to the riches of God's Glory the Ephesians would be strengthened with might by His Spirit in their inner man, that Christ may dwell in their hearts through faith"* (Ephesians 3:16 paraphrased). Considering it's weight we need strength to carry Glory.

Carrying the Glory is not so much that we contain the Glory, but rather that it contains us. He dwells in us but is not in any way limited by us. As St. Augustine contrasts, in the natural

Life In His Presence

realm the water in a cup is kept, held up, and contained by the vessel; however, it is in filling us that God keeps us, holds us up, and contains us. It's not so much that we are carrying the Glory, but rather that we are being carried by it. Jesus said to Nicodemus, *"the wind (the Spirit) blows wherever it pleases and no one knows where it comes from or where it goes, so it is with those who are born of the Spirit"* (paraphrase John 3:8). Those who carry the Glory are those who are carried by the wind of God.

When we carry the glory, the focus is not on us--not on how good or how skilled we are--but it is on the presence of God. In the glory, God is Glorified. We cannot take credit for anything that takes place in the Glory because we are neither deserving nor able to do any of the things that He does. *"For it is the God who commanded light to shine out of darkness, who has shone in our hearts to give the light of the knowledge of the glory of God in the face of Jesus Christ. But we have this treasure in earthen vessels, that the excellence of the power may be of God and not of us"* (2 Corinthians 4:6-7). We don't cause light, He does. We simply reflect Him, so that He may be known and glorified.

The Glory is mysterious and yet simple. It is exactly what it is called. It is the weighty reputation of God. It is His exaltation over all things. And it is also what brings Him Glory. Glory begets Glory. We need to remember this as we continue.

If we forget this, we may try to touch His Glory in order to make a good reputation for ourselves from the favor that comes in His presence. No one can touch His Glory. The man that tried to "save" the Ark of the covenant died as soon as he touched it, lest he walk away from that with the reputation of saving it. Glory is the exaltation of His Name and exists to exalt His Name rather than ours.

How to Carry the Glory

We already have access into the Holiest (Hebrews 10:19), and in a very real sense are already sitting in heavenly places in Christ Jesus (Ephesians 2:6). Christ, the hope of Glory is in us. The Holy Spirit is in us. Yet there is still an appropriating of these realities that only comes about in the context of Praise. It is in the praises of His people that God is enthroned (Psalm 22:3). Apart from those praises the weight of His would crush us.

A resting place for the presence of God was established in the Old Testament in a tabernacle filled with the incense of day and night Praise and Worship. In the tabernacle of David, there was constant worship and adoration in the presence of God that allowed the manifest presence of God (the Ark) and human beings to be in one place without people dying. In like manner, the resting place for the presence of God in the New Covenant is comprised of temples (we are the temple) filled

Life In His Presence

with the incense of Praise and Worship, day and night.

When we become praise to God, our lives a constant exaltation of His Name, we can live from a heavenly reality with the manifest presence of God on the Earth. We take hold of what has been freely given to us with mouths that are filled with praise.

When we enter His presence we won't want to go back to living a normal life. We want the Glory to permeate our lives and affect everything that we say and do. Essentially what God wants to do, and has been seeking to do since the beginning of time, is to "Shekinah" with man, that is, to dwell with man. He did it in the Garden, tried it with Israel in the desert, and will do it in a people that are a dwelling place for God in the Spirit (Ephesians 2:18-22). This is why I believe that the design of our procession into the Holy of Holies is primarily to be partaken of corporately, though it must also be sustained individually.

We can ascend the Hill of the Lord in one worship service and have a wonderful experience. This experience will fuel hunger for more of His presence and produce fruit in our hearts that comes from being in the presence of God. However, we don't have to come back down. We can become a people of praise!

This is why continual worship, the night and day incense of Malachi 1:11, makes sense. We can become a people who truly keep a throne of praise for the Lord at all times. For those in the Prayer movement, we can keep incense rising not just in the six or so hours we are in the prayer room each day but also in the ten or so other hours that we are awake. There are even those that have been known to pray and praise in their sleep! The Lord doesn't desire individuals alone within a community but a people, a whole community, on whose praises He can Shekinah.

As we wait upon the Lord, we can access the Glory of God in us. When we praise, the atmosphere around us gets filled with the manifest presence of God, and it is in that context that we will often linger and wait upon the Lord. What happens then is that His Glory begins to permeate our beings, till we are full and spilling over everywhere we go. As we participate in all these amazing disciplines with love and faith, we are filled with the Holy Spirit and become carriers of the Glory. Yes, the Holy Spirit is already in us. Yet as Paul encouraged the Ephesians, we can be continually filled with the Holy Spirit (Ephesians 5:18).

I believe there is more of His manifest presence available to fill us and that He comes in progressively. The train of His robe filled the temple in Isaiah 6. God was in the temple already and yet the temple was still being filled with His robe, more and more. We are the temple of the Holy Spirit and are to be continually filled with the Holy Spirit.

Life In His Presence

Jesus said to His disciples in John 16:12, *"I still have many things to say to you, but you cannot bear them now."* Their capacity to bear *"the good things to come"* (Hebrews 9:11; 10:1) that Jesus wanted to reveal and impart was non-existent apart from the Holy Spirit. Our capacity and strength to bear heavenly things will increase as we are filled with the Holy Spirit, as we are filled with the Glory (Ephesians 3:16-19).

Jesus said, *"I am the vine, you are the branches, he who abides in me and I in him, bears much fruit, for without Me you can do nothing"* (John 15:5). He did not say that those who abide in Him *will* bear much fruit, but that they already do. It is interesting that the word used here is "to bear or to carry" much fruit. That is the result of being near to Him, of abiding and dwelling in His House, of being in the Glory. We will begin to carry the fruit that is produced in His presence.

One of my mom's best friends is a worshipper who worships all the time and so is constantly in the presence of God. She has experienced many miracles, and whenever I've prayed for her to be healed of diverse afflictions, she has been healed, most times instantaneously. One time as we were worshipping together I prayed for her and she was healed of a headache. She then asked me to pray for her because she had a calcification in her breast. In the presence of God I commanded the calcification to leave her body and instantly she felt as if a hand had reached down and plucked it out! The mass left her body so that neither she nor the mammogram at the doctor's office could detect it! Praise the Lord!

She carries the presence of God, and in the Glory things are improved and healing is accelerated. Some of the greatest miracles I have personally witnessed have taken place in the manifest presence of God.

Vessels Prepared

There are two kinds of vessels God has prepared and is preparing for His Glory to indwell on the earth. One of them is the corporate body of believers and the other is individuals that know Him and love Him. We are new creations, made as temples to carry the manifest presence of God, both as individuals and as a people who are *being built together for a dwelling place of God in the Spirit* (Ephesians 2:20-22).

Paul writes in two different chapters and contexts in 1 Corinthians that we are temples of the Holy Spirit. In chapter 3 he is writing about the church body being a temple, and in chapter 6 he is writing about individuals' bodies being temples of the Holy Spirit. God likes bodies and has decided to have His Glory dwell in them.

In the Old Testament Moses carried the Glory on him as an individual when he came down from the mountain but it faded. Now God wants all of us to carry His ever-increasing and never-fading Glory. The rest of the children of Israel were

Life In His Presence

unable to willingly host His presence as a corporate people because they did not trust Him. God dwelt among them but Moses had to plead with Him that He would actually remain with them (Exodus 33).

Carrying the Glory: A Corporate Reality

Carrying the Glory of God is something that God designed for a corporate people to do. Paul expresses this design to the Ephesians when he wrote:

"Now, therefore, you are no longer strangers and foreigners, but fellow citizens with the saints and members of the household of God, having been built on the foundation of the apostles and prophets, Jesus Christ Himself being the chief cornerstone, in whom the whole building, being fitted together, grows into a holy temple in the Lord, in whom you also are being built together for a dwelling place of God in the Spirit."

Ephesians 2:19-22

God had this concept in mind for the children of Israel as they wandered through the wilderness and He was preparing them so that He could Shekinah (dwell) with them, but they did not know His ways and rejected His invitation. The presence of God would constantly manifest among them as God drew near to them. They did not know His ways, hardened their hearts, and did not obey His Word through unbelief. *"For the gospel was preached to us as well as to them; but the word which they heard did not profit them, not being mixed with faith in those who heard it"* (Hebrews 4:2). Therefore He swore in His wrath, because of their unbelief, that they would not enter His rest. All of them died in the wilderness except Joshua and Caleb, the only two who believed God's Word.

The LORD has desired to Shekinah with man throughout all of human history, starting from Adam and Eve, to Abraham who desired a heavenly city (Hebrews 11:10), to Moses' tabernacle, to David's Tabernacle, to the temple of Solomon, to the Word made flesh and dwelling among us (John 1:14), to the day of Pentecost, to the city of Samaria receiving the Holy Spirit as Peter and John laid hands on them (Acts 8), to Cornelius and his household being filled with the Holy Spirit (Acts 10), to the revival in Antioch and in Ephesus, to the Moravian Pentecost, to the Great Awakenings, to Maria Woodworth Etter's meetings, to the Azusa Street Revival, to the Voice of Healing, to the Jesus Movement, to the revivals in the 80's and 90's, to the revival in Mozambique with Heidi Baker, to the prayer movement, to other revivals, and all the way to the time when He will fulfill this desire. Jesus will return to earth and the Father will be enthroned amongst His people in the Holy City forever.

Life In His Presence

God's desire is for a people that will walk as one in His power and presence. As described in the early chapters of the book of Acts, the entire city respected and feared the church: *"And through the hands of the apostles many signs and wonders were done among the people. And they were all with one accord in Solomon's Porch. Yet none of the rest dared join them, but the people esteemed them highly"* (Acts 5:12-13). And this is still available to a people who will with one accord seek His Face and cry out like Moses, "Lord, show me Your Glory."

The church in Jerusalem carried His presence to such an extent that the people around them were filled with the fear of the Lord. The signs and wonders, Ananias' and Sapphira's deaths, and the men at Pentecost appearing as though they were drunk were not the cause of the Fear of the Lord (though some of those events were pretty scary); it was the Spirit of God who caused those signs that brought forth the Fear of the Lord in the city. Wherever one of them walked, the people knew he was a part of the church because of the presence of God that rested upon the corporate body. Others knew the person was part of the church because of the presence of God that rested upon him, not because of the shirt he was wearing or because he sounded Christian or looked Christian or told anyone he was Christian. The people of the region would recognize the presence and thereby esteem them.

Acts 5 tells of the consequence of a people that were full of the Glory: increase and multitudes. *"And believers were increasingly added to the Lord, multitudes of both men and women"* (Acts 5:14). This was the increase that came about and yet only the Apostles are mentioned as the ones doing the signs and the wonders. The presence of God on a corporate people can and will influence a region. The truth will be exalted, and freedom will be released. The Glory will cast down lofty thoughts that exalt themselves above the knowledge of God and turn a hardened people into those who fear the Lord.

There have been times in history where people have flocked to the church as the presence of God was manifest. We see it all over Acts. In the day of Pentecost three thousand were added. During the Azusa Street Revival many turned to Jesus. These have been sovereign moves of God on His people, yet there was human participation in these. I believe we have access to enter into and carry that same presence. Presently most of what we see in the West is people going from church to church, from meeting to meeting. Oh for the day when the Glory so rests on a corporate people, and even upon individuals, that sinners would be swept into the Kingdom, being drawn by the sound (Acts 2), by the fame of Jesus, by the Glory of the Lord.

On the day of Pentecost *"there came a <u>sound</u> from heaven as of a mighty rushing wind"* (Acts 2:2). There was a sound that was released. The word for sound in the Greek is the

Life In His Presence

word *echos,* which means "rumor, fame, or sound." This is where we get the word echo. There came an *echos* from heaven--a rumor, fame. So what happened? People flocked to it.

This fame that was manifested over and expressed through a corporate people drew the multitudes. Those who are echoed in the world are those who have a level of fame. In the early church and to this day, His spread and echoed throughout that region and throughout the regions of the earth.

Carrying the Glory: An Individual Expression

The echo came forth from a corporate people, a dwelling place for God, a temple. The church was walking in the manifest presence of God and many were coming to the Lord. The church was increasingly being added to as it carried the presence. As a corporate people, they "had it going on"! They had a unity that was unparalleled in their time--though it will be surpassed (Ephesians 4:11-13)--and together were feared by the region. At that point only a select few of them had the reputation of being full of the Holy Spirit and fewer still were appropriating many of the riches that were available in that Glory, but I believe that all, not just the apostles, were meant to be full of the Spirit and even meant to be empowered witnesses.

There is a great benefit to being full of the Holy Spirit that impacts people, places, and even regions. Without the person doing anything, except being a praise for the Lord, they see a change to their environment. When individuals don't just wait for the next Sunday service to show their love to Jesus, but become an expression of love for the Lord, then they begin to carry His presence everywhere they go. This is a powerful reality, and I believe it is available to all who are hungry and thirsty for the Lord. This is carrying the glory.

It is easy when among a community of fiery believers, to go along with the corporate flowing of the Holy Spirit while never actually entering into a personal living encounter with God, into an encounter that not only transforms us, but also sets our heart in pursuit of the Lord for the rest of our lives. It is easy to get caught up in emotion around those who love the Lord and yet not be empowered ourselves to carry and release that transformation to others. We cannot depend on someone else's relationship and zeal for the Lord; we ourselves need to go before Him in the secret place. A good example of what I am trying to articulate can be seen in the life of King Saul. He got around the prophets and he prophesied. But his lifestyle did not change and did not come in line with the Word of God.

We need more than anointed church services, more than a crowd that knows how to flow with the Spirit. What we need is a generation that will seek the Lord, laying down their lives in pursuit of Him (Hebrew 12:1-2). Again, it's easy to look spiritual, act spiritual, and even do supernatural things and yet not really be hosting the presence of God in our individual

Life In His Presence

lives. Judas had healed the sick and performed signs yet he betrayed Jesus. If we ride on someone else's anointing but never get the oil of intimacy for ourselves (Matthew 25) then we are not really carrying the Glory, nor are we really abiding in the vine. Some of us have deceived ourselves to think that because we saw the power of God flowing through us we had an intimate knowledge of God that we never went to the secret place to acquire. If we do not have intimacy with God, we will see that we are really dry and barren when we are no longer around the powerful ministry, conference, group, etc. Then we will see that the anointing in which we were operating was not our own.

Many see God move powerfully when they are involved in mission trips, in powerful conferences, or in powerful churches. Some will find after they are away from those events or groups that they no longer walk in the same grace they experienced around the fire. I am not claiming to have full understanding for the lack of effectiveness experienced while away from such communities but there are many reasons that I can think of: God may remove the feeling and even grace to draw you to Himself so that you may seek Him, the people you ministered to then had faith and were not doubtful, or God may have called you to go there specifically and therefore gave you what you needed for the specific task. There may be many reasons for the lack of power, but I want to highlight that perhaps we were operating on someone else's anointing rather than in our own. The solution then may be as simple as just needing to be with God. He does not want to use robots; though He will even use donkeys if He has to and has certainly used dry believers. However, He wants to use lovers. The Holy Spirit is not an emotionless power that fills us--He is God. If you want to be filled with the Holy Spirit, I advise that you spend time with Him.

Doing What the Father is Doing

There is even more! The Spirit of the Lord came upon Jesus and empowered Him to do mighty works so that He could fulfill the call and ministry on His life. Peter declared, as he preached after the Holy Spirit came upon the apostles, that Jesus did the works that He did as a man. He needed the power of the Holy Spirit to do the works. Jesus also said that He would only do what He saw the Father doing. *Then Jesus answered and said to them, "Most assuredly, I say to you, the Son can do nothing of Himself, but what He sees the Father do; for whatever He does, the Son also does in like manner"* (John 5:19). Not only can we carry the presence of God, but we can also participate with what we see the Father doing in the Glory.

In this next section we will dive more into our appropriation of the grace for advancing the Kingdom (Luke 11:20) through the works Christ did. There is grace available in

Life In His Presence

His presence for the Anointing to be upon us and not just within us (Isaiah 61). We need it within us, but the world needs it upon us. Bill Johnson says it this way, "The Holy Spirit is in you for your sake, He is upon you for the sake of others." An individual can be carrying the resident Glory of the Holy Spirit within him, but not be clothed with power to do the works of Jesus.

"The Spirit of the Lord GOD is upon me, because the LORD has anointed me to bring good news to the poor; he has sent me to bind up the brokenhearted, to proclaim liberty to the captives, and the opening of the prison to those who are bound."

Isaiah 61:1

The Apostle Peter was an individual carrying the Glory and overflowing. Acts 5 tells of what happened when he walked down the street: *"So that they brought the sick out into the streets and laid them on beds and couches, that at least the shadow of Peter passing by might fall on some of them. Also a multitude gathered from the surrounding cities to Jerusalem bringing sick people and those who were tormented by unclean sprits, and they were all healed"* (Acts 5:15-16).

The early church was revered and feared because of the Glory that rested on it (Acts 5 & 6). Some were *"Full of the Holy Spirit and wisdom"* (Acts 6:3) but were not yet walking in the power as witnesses. There were those who operated in their calling and ministry from the Glory, who accessed and utilized resources from another age, resources from the Glory. These three groups were the church as a corporate body, the Seven that were full of the Holy Spirit and were chosen to wait tables (Acts 6), and the Apostles.

At this point in the church many, if not all, were filled with the Holy Spirit and some are described as being full of the Holy Spirit. The individuals full of the Spirit were carrying the Glory and were obviously, according to the text, distinguishable in the church. Although the church as a whole was corporately carrying the manifest presence, these seven had a reputation among believers of being "Full of the Spirit." However, there is a sense that even these had not yet been released into a greater dimension of the power of God, of the Anointing upon them.

The Apostles, those in full-time ministry, were obviously carrying the Glory and making withdrawals from its treasury. They were operating in their calling and ministry from a place of continual intimacy and encounter with God. The overflow of their intimacy with the Lord permeated out of them as a fragrance affecting all those who were around to smell it. *"Now thanks be to God who always leads us in triumph in Christ, and through us diffuses the fragrance of His knowledge in every place"* (2 Corinthians 2:14).

Life In His Presence

The presence of God was manifest, but only the Apostles were spilling over. This assumption comes from the fact that no one except the apostles is mentioned to perform signs and wonders until the Seven, those in the work place full of the Holy Spirit, were raised up. One hundred and twenty had been filled with the Holy Spirit and thousands of others afterward, but the Scriptures specify only eleven, maybe twelve, through whom signs and wonders were performed. This is not at all to imply that the apostles or the early church were doing anything wrong. I believe that they were exactly where God wanted them. They were following the Holy Spirit through the diverse circumstances that came up and God was setting them up for multiplication. My point is that at this time the Five-fold Apostles, those who are called by God to lead and equip the church, were the ones primarily walking in the greater works (Ephesians 4:11-14).

Problems arose in the church when the Apostles found themselves in the predicament of having to "serve tables" in addition to their main responsibility to the Word of God and prayer. They had the people pick seven men from among themselves who were full of the Holy Spirit and wisdom whom they would appoint to that business (Acts 6:1-6). *"And they chose Stephen, a man full of faith and the Holy Spirit, and Philip, Prochorus, Nicanor, Timon, Parmenas, and Nicolas…" (Acts 6:5). After the Apostles laid hands on them, it says, "Then the word of God spread, and the number of the disciples multiplied greatly in Jerusalem..."* (Acts 6:7). In the verses and chapters following, we find that now no longer was it the Apostles alone walking in the power. The church began, in a wider scale, to walk in the authority that had been given to it. They began to appropriate the eternal resources in the riches of His Glory (Ephesians 3:16).

The Apostles were led of the Holy Spirit to equip the saints for the work of ministry (Ephesians 4:11-13) by the laying-on of their hands. From there we began to see other saints doing what they saw the Father doing. What happened when the church carrying the presence began to exercise the power present in them? In Acts 5:14 where the Apostles alone are mentioned to be doing the works, it says, *"Believers were increasingly added to the Lord."* Now in Acts 6:7, as more of the church was released to walk in the greater works, it says, *"The disciples multiplied greatly in Jerusalem."*

Appropriating the Treasures of His Glory

Throughout the Scriptures God often chooses to use people to release individuals into their calling. Even Jesus Himself was released after John the Baptist baptized Him, then the Holy Spirit came upon Him (Matthew 3:14-17). Prophets often anointed kings before they became kings. Sometimes individuals will be unable to step into all that God has for them apart from those who will release them. This was not always the case, as we see with some of the judges, including Samuel who received the anointing and was released into it by being before the Ark. We do not know if anyone anointed Elijah or John the Baptist, for example. But in the book of Acts, we see that God chose to use men to bring the Seven into God's purposes for their lives.

There are people who are very full of the Spirit because they spend hours with the Lord, and others know it because we can sense His presence on them. They carry the presence and there is creative potential around them, but they don't know how to step into all that is available in His Glory for His Glory. Some don't even know that stepping into it is an option. They carry the Glory more than many people I know who prophesy accurately, heal the sick, etc. I love to be around them. They are awesome, sensitive to the Spirit, full of faith and the Holy Spirit. Their life in the secret place brings Glory to God.

The same was the case in the early church where the Holy Spirit led the apostles to raise up the Seven and to lay hands on them. The apostles were not aware of what that would accomplish, but the Holy Spirit knew very well what it would produce. They were mainly aware of the practical need for administrators and were not as aware that the Lord intended for these also to preach the gospel with boldness, with signs and wonders following, and that multiplication would result. These businessmen were used with the power of the Holy Spirit as witnesses.

When the Apostles laid hands on the Seven, they were functioning in their calling to equip the saints and were releasing those Seven to walk in a level of power and authority they had not yet tapped into. We need equipping like that today; we need the body to be equipped to do the works of ministry. I know of churches and ministries where congregations look to the pastors and spiritual leaders alone to minister to them for healing, deliverance, etc. These are things that I believe the Lord intends for all believers to walk in. I wonder what will happen if Five-fold ministers begin to equip and release these precious saints for the work of ministry (Ephesians 4:12).

I have been focusing greatly on the supernatural works that Jesus did and gave us access to do. He did these works to bring Glory to His Father and to validate that He spoke not on His own authority but on the Authority of the Father (John 7:16-18). He said that if He cast out devils by the finger of God then the Kingdom of God had come upon them (Luke 11:20). It was with these works that He would advance the Kingdom of Heaven on the earth. This is not to say that those who are not in full-time ministry cannot be used powerfully by God. For example, school teachers can function in the power of the Holy Spirit within their gifting to teach and set the captives free.

Life In His Presence

Jesus speaks of the anointing of the Spirit being upon Himself, and to the same anointing He has invited us—the Seven-Fold Spirit of God resting on believers. This I believe is what the Lord is trying to highlight about carrying the Glory. The Spirit came upon Jesus and remained (Shekinah) so that Jesus carried the presence wherever He went. Likewise, we are to be full of the Spirit and to carry the Spirit of Wisdom and Understanding, of Counsel and Might, of Knowledge and of the Fear of the Lord, the Spirit of the Lord (Isaiah 11) upon us no matter where we go. Why do we need this? So that we can manifest His power wherever we go. So that the school teacher can lay hands on her student that has a cough and the cough will leave; that while she teaches math, the presence of God fills the room to release joy and freedom. So that while a secretary does her job, peace fills the office, etc. It is not whether a person's gifting can work the works Jesus did, for the Glory goes beyond gifting and knowledge into the manifestation of what the Father is doing.

Another aspect to appropriating what is available for believers is having faith in, and understanding of, the Word. Receiving by faith the things that the scriptures say we will do is a very practical way to access what is available. Individuals can carry the presence of the Lord around them and yet not always know to appropriate all that is available in it. We can walk around with batteries, but if we don't know that we can put them in a flashlight to dispel darkness, we might not get as far as we would if we knew what we could do with them. Anyone that is full of the Spirit will impact atmospheres and carry freedom with them, *"for where the Spirit of the Lord is there is freedom"* (2 Corinthians 3:17). Their prayers will be powerful and their countenance alone will lift others up. With wisdom and revelation, however, we will know those things that have been freely given to us.

"For we have not received the spirit of the world but the Spirit which is from God, that we may know the things that have been freely given to us." We have received the Spirit of Wisdom and Revelation. We have access through faith, and through wisdom and understanding we know what we have access to and can take hold of it.

There is a tension. We have already been blessed with every spiritual blessing in the heavenly places in Christ, yet there is an equipping and an empowering, and God uses people or divine means as the access into some of those blessings that have been freely given. God used Samuel to anoint David to be king over Israel (1 Samuel 16). Moses encountered the Angel of the Lord and was anointed and commissioned into his purpose and destiny as a deliverer to lead the Israelites out of Egypt (Exodus 3). What God is imparting through people or other divine means we cannot otherwise step into. If it is true that with wisdom and revelation we can access things that have been

Life In His Presence

freely given to us--and it is true--then why did Stephen and Phillip who were already full of wisdom need the Apostles to lay hands on them, to walk in greater power and authority? Is it that they received something that they did not already have access to? Or is the Way, the access to those things, in submission to leadership and in patience for God's providence? There are things that we cannot access apart from submission to leadership, apart from partaking of His fruits and character, apart from walking in His Way.

There certainly is a calling on the five-fold ministry to equip the saints (Ephesians 4), and I believe much of that equipping is showing the saints what is already theirs. It is also imparting what has been freely given to them. Jesus said to the Apostles, freely you have received now freely give (Matthew 10:8). John the Baptist said that a man only has what he has received from heaven (John 3:27). The Lord distributes gifts by His Spirit and through others. The Apostles laid hands on Samaritans who then received the Holy Spirit (Acts 8).

"Are all apostles? Are all prophets? Are all teachers? Are all workers of miracles? Do all have gifts of healings? Do all speak with tongues? Do all interpret? But earnestly desire the best gifts. And yet I show you a more excellent way" (1 Corinthians 12:29-31). Not everyone walks in every gift, but we certainly have permission, and it is our responsibility, to earnestly desire them. Yet in His presence, we can step into His

gifting and His anointing in order to bring glory to His Name.

His presence is Holy

As I mentioned in the beginning of this chapter, the manifest presence of God destroyed the lives of thousands of people who profaned the Lord out of disobedience or ignorance. This very presence is the One that we are excited about carrying in earthen vessels and privileged to carry. One thing we must understand in this is that His presence is Holy. Even in the New Covenant it is still a fearful thing to fall into the hands of the living God (Hebrews 10:31).

This Holy presence requires nothing less than Holiness for us to enter in. This has not changed from the Old Covenant. Praise God that He has made Holiness available to us through the Blood of His Son Jesus. This is the beauty of the New Covenant. But if our hearts are not in agreement with His righteousness, and our hearts are unrepentant, then it will be impossible for us to enter into and carry this weighty presence. There is only One way into the Holy Place, and it is through the Cross. The new and living way that Christ prepared for us is a consecrated way (Hebrews 10:20). We receive the finished work by becoming crucified with Christ so that no longer is it us that live, but Christ in us (Galatians 2:20).

Toleration of sin is not acceptable in the Glory. No sin is a small sin and is certainly not seen as such in the presence of

Life In His Presence

God but is fully deserving of Judgment. If we are in conscious agreement with a certain sin, regardless of how small it seems, then we are not partaking of the Righteousness of Christ and are in need of repentance. The Blood of Jesus does not cover willingly unrepentant sin.

Earlier in this chapter I mentioned the 3rd and 6th chapters of 1 Corinthians. These are chapters in which Paul explains to the Corinthians that they as the Church are the temple of the Holy Spirit, and that they as individuals are temples of the Holy Spirit. Surrounding these explanations are admonitions to stay away from the wisdom of this age, which brings division to the church, and to flee sexual immorality. These were sins that they were in conscious agreement with or were tolerating in each other. James called the wisdom of this age, *"earthly, sensual, and demonic. For where envy and self-seeking exist, confusion and every evil thing are there"* (James 3:15-16). The author of Hebrews gives us the key to Carrying the Glory corporately and individually when he writes *"Pursue peace with all people, and Holiness, without which no one will see the Lord"* (Hebrews 12:14). These are the issues that Paul addresses with the Corinthians that threatened their privilege to host the Holy Spirit as His temples. Disunity and Impurity are of the greatest threats to Carrying the Glory.

The design that the Builder chose to use for His presence to dwell among men has a key component-- "together." *"Christ*

Carrying the Glory   *Chapter 3*

Himself being the chief cornerstone, in whom the whole building, being fitted <u>together</u>, grows into a holy temple in the Lord, in whom you also are being built <u>together</u> for a dwelling place of God in the Spirit" (Ephesians 2:20b-22). How blessed it is when we worship the Lord together in one accord. It is in that context that the anointing, the Glory, falls upon us and drips down (Psalm 133).

In the Glory there is no room for disunity nor is there room for immorality. If you desire to carry the Glory and find that there is agreement with these in your heart, simply repent. Humble yourself by admitting your fault, turn to Jesus to set you free, and get in His presence. This doesn't mean that we have to make ourselves perfect in order to experience and love God and in order to host His presence. By the Blood of Jesus we are being perfected and are perfect before the Father. But it does mean that we have to humble ourselves to receive that righteousness and we have to trust the Lord to deliver us from what we come out of agreement with.

This Glory that we desire to carry is not our own but God's. If we seek our own glory, we will begin to carry confusion and every evil thing (James 3:16). It is as scary as it sounds. There are great benefits for us when we are in His presence. Even these can be a hindrance to us if we turn our gaze from the Beautiful One and His Glory to our own promotion. The Israelites were admonished of this by Moses in

Life In His Presence

Deuteronomy 6-8: *"Lest – when you have eaten and are full, and have built beautiful houses and dwell in them; and when your herds and your flocks multiply, and your silver and your gold are multiplied, and all that you have is multiplied; when your heart is lifted up, and you forget the LORD your God who brought you out of the land of Egypt, from the house of bondage..."* (Deuteronomy 8:12-14).

So I will conclude this chapter with the words of James: *"But if you have bitter envy and self-seeking in your hearts, do not boast against the truth. This wisdom does not descend from above, but is earthly, sensual, demonic. For where envy and self-seeking exist, confusion and every evil thing are there. But the wisdom that is from above is first pure, then peaceable, gentle, willing to yield, full of mercy and good fruits, without hypocrisy. Now the fruit of righteousness is sown in peace by those who make peace"* (James 3:14-18).

Chapter 4

The Ark of the Covenant

In the Old Testament God commanded Moses to build the Ark of the Testimony. In it were placed the tablets of the covenant, a golden pot with manna, and Aaron's rod that budded. It was overlaid on all sides with gold (Exodus 25, Hebrews 9:4). In this box God put His presence. Anywhere the Ark went, the manifest presence of God went with it. It did not contain God, who is everywhere, or restrict God. When the Ark was not in Israel, God still spoke to Samuel; when it wasn't in Jerusalem, He still used David to kill Goliath. But the presence of God was on the Ark, it was consecrated to the Lord, and He did what He pleased with it.

This Box was a shadow of what was on the Lord's heart for humanity. It carried the presence of God. To the children of Israel it represented and manifested the presence of God. It was designed to be kept in a place where only Holiness had access, The Holy of Holies. Most of the time, few people even had

Life In His Presence

access to see it. Under the old covenant, in the priestly function, the high priest saw it once a year when he went behind the veil into the Holiest of All to atone for the sins of the people. Through the blood of Jesus we can have boldness to enter the Holiest (Hebrews 10:19). Now we have a hope that *"enters the presence behind the veil"* (Hebrews 6:19). Now we, as new creations, are designed to host the presence just as the Ark of the Covenant did, and even more so. Now in Christ, we are one spirit with God and are to be carriers of the Glory.

We can get an idea from Israel's experience of what is the benefit and severity of carrying the Glory or of being near to Him. God actually warned Moses about Him destroying the people if He continued with them. Many times plagues broke out against the people, killing thousands because of their sin in the presence of God (Exodus 33; Numbers 11, 16). An offense against a King is greater the closer you are to Him, and the recompense more immediate. However, one major difference between those times and these is that we are covered by the blood of Jesus. Much of the severity that was experienced by Israel and surrounding nations was because of their unrighteousness. In the last plague to Egypt a distinction is given between those covered by the Blood and those who are not. In times past they experienced God as unrighteous men, but now we come before Him as new creations, as the righteousness of God in Christ.

The Ark of the Covenant   *Chapter 4*

The Ark

On Mount Sinai the LORD told Moses to build an Ark of acacia wood and overlay it with gold on every side (Exodus 25). It would have the Mercy seat with cherubim surrounding the top of the Ark. Also the Testimony was to be placed within the Ark. Four golden rings were cast and put on the four corners of the Ark and poles of acacia wood were overlaid with gold to put them through the rings in order to carry the Ark. The Ark was to be placed in the Tabernacle of Testimony behind veils in the Most Holy.

Moses was told to make everything according to the blueprint shown to him on the mountain, and out of it came an Ark with a picture of the Throne Room in Heaven set on top of it.

The Ark on earth represented a heavenly reality. On top of the Ark were the Mercy seat and the two cherubim of Glory. Around God's Throne there are angels that never cease crying "Holy, Holy, Holy," and in the Ark we have a picture of this on the earth. Furthermore, God designed it so that at the center of His Glory is the expression of His Mercy. Even this, I believe, was a foreshadowing of the Cross. God told Moses that He would speak with him from the top of the Mercy seat.

"Now on the day that the tabernacle was raised up, the cloud covered the Tabernacle, the tent of the Testimony; from evening

Life In His Presence

until morning it was above the tabernacle like the appearance of fire. So it was always; the cloud covered it by day, and the appearance of fire by night. Whenever the cloud was taken up from above the tabernacle, after that the children of Israel would journey; and in the place where the cloud settled, there the children of Israel would pitch their tents."

Numbers 9:15-18

Keeping the Charge of the Lord

"Whether it was two days, a month, or a year that the cloud remained above the tabernacle, the children of Israel would remain encamped and not journey; but when it was taken up, they would journey. At the command of the LORD they remained encamped, and at the command of the LORD they journeyed; they kept the charge of the LORD, at the command of the LORD by the hand of Moses.

Numbers 9:22-23

The Children were to keep the charge of the Lord. The word "charge" in the Hebrew is *mishmereth,* which also means "watch." The children of Israel had to keep the ordinance that the LORD gave to them, which was to follow the Cloud. In order to do so, they had to keep watching the cloud and paying attention so that they moved when it moved and they settled where it settled.

I believe that these verses are a key to priestly ministry, to the keeping of the altar. It was when the manifest Glory remained in their midst that they would set up the Tabernacle of the Testimony. The ministry before the LORD in which they participated was not absent of His manifest presence.

Crossing the Jordan

The Lord always made a way for the Children of Israel to obey His command. Most, if not all, of His commands were things that they could not possibly do, yet He commanded them to do so. He wanted them to rely on Him and wanted to teach them that *"Man shall not live by bread alone"* (Matthew 4:4)-- by the things that man's own hand could provide--but by obedience to every Word that proceeds from the mouth of God. As they walked in step with His Spirit, the obstacles would be removed and the limitations would cease to be.

Several million people were expected to cross the Jordan River with children, livestock, supplies, etc. God commanded that the priests should go first with the Ark. *"And it shall come to pass, as soon as the soles of the feet of the priests who bear the Ark of the covenant of the LORD, the lord of all the earth, shall rest in the waters of the Jordan, that the waters of the Jordan shall be cut off, the waters that come down from upstream, and they shall stand as a heap... [they] stood on dry ground in the midst of the Jordan; and all Israel crossed over*

Life In His Presence

on dry ground, until all the people had crossed completely over the Jordan" (Joshua 3:13,17).

The Wall of Jericho

"See! I have given Jericho into your hand, its king, and the mighty men of valor. You shall march around the city, all you men of war; you shall go all around the city once. This you shall do six days. And seven priests shall bear seven trumpets of rams' horns before the Ark. But the seventh day you shall march around the city seven times, and the priests shall blow the trumpets. It shall come to pass, when they make a long blast with the ram's horn, and when you hear the sound of the trumpet, that all the people shall shout with a great shout; then the wall of the city will fall down flat, and the people shall go up every man straight before him."

Joshua 6:1-5

When the LORD commanded Israel to march around the walls of Jericho, He gave them specific directions on what they were to do, one of them being to carry the Ark with them around the walls. Our greatest strategy against the enemy is to carry the presence of God, to usher in the rule and dominion of the King.

The praises of His people are His throne; His enemies are His footstool (Psalm 110). I can see the walls of Jericho being unable to bear the weight of His feet as the children of Israel raised a shout of Praise to God. The LORD commands them to praise, to "ter-oo-aw'" (Joshua 6:5). They were to "roo-ah" (split the ears, make a joyful noise) with a great "ter-oo-aw'" (loud noise, rejoicing, shouting, high and joyful sound). Anything that stands in opposition to His rule and dominion will be crushed by the Kabod, just as the walls of Jericho fell down flat.

It is interesting that God makes mention of the priests who were to carry and blow the trumpets, the mighty men of war, and Joshua, but He does not make mention of the priests who would carry the Ark. He mentions the Ark but not the people who would be carrying it. His lack of mentioning them was not because He didn't like them, or because they were bad people, or because He liked those whom He did mention more. Not at all. They were not mentioned because the Ark was filled with His glory--it's all about HIS Glory.

Samuel

Samuel was dedicated to the LORD from the time He was weaned (1 Samuel 1:24). He ministered to the Lord and lay before the Ark. The Lord established him as a prophet in Israel and his words did not fall to the ground. Even after the Ark was taken away, he himself had communion and connection with God. He himself became a carrier of the Glory.

Life In His Presence

Philistine Temple and Cities

During Eli's time, Israel fought against the Philistines and lost a battle. The Hebrews brought the Ark from Shiloh with them into battle, as a good luck charm, though they were walking in unrighteousness before the Lord. They said *"Why has the LORD defeated us today before the Philistines? Let us bring the Ark of the covenant of the LORD from Shiloh to us, that when it comes among us it may save us from the hand of our enemies"* (1 Samuel 4:4).

They also lost that battle, and the Philistines took the Ark with them. *"When the Philistines took the Ark of God, they brought it into the house of Dagon and set it by Dagon* (their chief god). *And when the people of Ashdod arose early in the morning, there was Dagon, fallen on its face to the earth before the Ark of the LORD. So they took Dagon and set it in its place again. And when they arose early the next morning, there was Dagon, fallen on its face to the ground before the Ark of the LORD. The head of Dagon and both the palms of its hands were broken off on the threshold; only Dagon's torso was left of it...* (1 Samuel 5:2-4).

But the hand of the LORD WAS HEAVY ON THE PEOPLE OF Ashdod, and He ravaged them and struck them with tumors, both Ashdod and its territory. And when the men of Ashdod saw how it was, they said, "The Ark of the God of Israel must not remain with us, for His hand is harsh toward us and Dagon our god."

1 Samuel 5:6-7

"... for there was deadly destruction throughout all the city; the hand of God was very heavy there. And the men who did not die were stricken with the tumors…"

1 Samuel 5:11b-12a

So it was in every other city of the Philistines in which the Ark was carried to.

Return to Israel

When the Philistines could not take it any longer, they sent the Ark back to Israel with five golden rats and five golden tumors. They recognized that they were dealing with a holy God that was against them, and they did not want to continue under His heavy hand. Up to that point the Ark had always been carried by priests. The Philistines did not know how to handle the Holy, as Tommy Tenney would say, and were not fit to do so. So they sent it back on a cart pulled by two milk cows that had never been yoked. Their priests and diviners told them that if the cows pulled the cart to Beth Shemesh then it was the LORD's hand against them and if it went the other direction then it happened to them by chance. The LORD actually led the

Life In His Presence

cows to Beth Shemesh and had them stop at the field of Joshua in front of a large rock. When the people of Israel saw it, they rejoiced and used the wood of the cart to make a fire and sacrificed the cows as burnt offerings.

After the people in Beth Shemesh had celebrated with sacrifices and the Levites had placed the Ark on top of a large stone, *"He struck the men of Beth Shemesh, because they had looked into the Ark of the Lord. He struck fifty thousand and seventy men of the people, and the people lamented because the LORD had struck the people with a great slaughter. And the men of Beth Shemesh said, 'Who is able to stand before this holy LORD God? And to whom shall it go up from us?'"* (1 Samuel 6:19-20). The people of Beth Shemesh also did not know how to handle the Holy. Israel was in a backslidden state when the Ark returned to them. They, being impure, looked into the manifest presence of God, but there was nothing to mediate between them and the raw power of God.

House of Obed-Edom

When David was bringing the Ark back with him to Jerusalem, like the Philistines did, they put the Ark that was meant to be carried by priests on a new cart pulled by oxen. This didn't work very well; when the oxen stumbled, Uzzah tried to save the Glory and was struck dead. I believe there was a little bit more involved here than a man trying to keep a box

The Ark of the Covenant　　　　　　　　　　　　　　*Chapter 4*

on a cart. I believe this is one example of touching His Glory--as if God needs to be protected! These are just some of my own thoughts as I studied this scripture.

David feared bringing the Ark with him to Jerusalem and left it at Obed-Edom's house for three months. Obed-Edom was blessed--and it must have been significantly--for the news of it reached King David.

"The Ark of the LORD remained in the house of Obed-Edom the Gittite three months. And the LORD blessed Obed-Edom and all his household. Now it was told King David, saying, 'The LORD has blessed the house of Obed-Edom and all that belongs to him, because of the Ark of God.' So David went and brought up the Ark of God from the house of Obed-Edom to the City of David with gladness."

2 Samuel 6:11-12

When David heard the news of how Obed-Edom had been blessed, he decided that having the Ark with him would be a good idea. When he went to retrieve the Ark, he took with him many priests clothed in priestly garments. He himself wore priestly garments (1 Chronicles 15:27). And he said, *"No one may carry the Ark of God but the Levites, for the LORD has chosen them to carry the Ark of God and to minister before Him forever"* (1 Chronicles 15:2). He had the right idea and, as the

Life In His Presence

priests carried the Ark, there was praise and celebration all around it.

David's Tabernacle

What is interesting about the Tabernacle of David is that, though the Mosaic law was still in full effect, David erected a tabernacle that did not follow the model Moses was given. In that tabernacle he put the Ark until David's son Solomon would build a resting place for the Ark. David confidently stepped into things from another age. There in the tabernacle that David erected, worshippers would worship before the Ark without the great divide that was experienced in Moses' Tabernacle. The perennial worship that would rise like incense before the Ark in that tent made it possible for people to be in the presence of a Holy God. The continual praises, like a throne, carried the weight of His Glory so that the priests could live and serve in His manifest presence.

Unlike those in Beth Shemesh who died, worshippers now had something to stand between them and the raw power of God. They had the incense of night and day praise and worship. Still, no one would want to make the mistake of touching it. In this tabernacle many of the Psalms were written, and to this day there is a glorious anointing on the Psalms.

Blessing and Judgment

There are great benefits to being in the presence of the One who created the universe and who loves us. There is a great benefit just in being in His House. David so desired this experience of being with God that he continually meditated on the dwelling place of God and joyfully contemplated his eternal home. *"Surely goodness and mercy shall follow (râdaph - run after; chase; hunt; pursue) me all the days of my life; and I will dwell in the house of the LORD forever"* (Psalm 23:6).

When we dwell in the house of the Lord, in the place where His Glory dwells (Psalm 26:8), not only will we have Goodness and Mercy but also they will follow us and pursue us. He Himself is Goodness and Mercy. This is what begins to happen as we are continually before the Lord. As we are *"still praising Him"* (Psalm 84:4), we dwell in His house forever. David said that one day in the courts of the Lord is better than a thousand days elsewhere (Psalm 84:10). It is more fruitful and more refreshing in His house than anywhere else, for goodness and mercy follow.

Those in opposition to God don't want anything to do with His presence because it is destructive to their schemes and plans. It dethrones wickedness and shakes all that can be shaken. The Philistines soon found out about the danger of being in the presence of Him whose Ways they despised. However, those who are of a broken heart and a contrite Spirit

Life In His Presence

find the delights that are in His presence (Psalm 16) and get to drink of His River (Psalm 36 and 46). The man with whom King David left the Ark after his first attempt to bring the Ark to Jerusalem prospered and flourished in the presence of the Almighty. It is interesting that they failed in their first attempt because they did not know how to carry the Glory. They placed it on a cart pulled by cows instead of having priests carry it as God commanded (Exodus 25:12-14). The presence of God is meant to be carried by image-bearers, by those who are made in His image (Genesis 1:26). That incident also serves as a lesson to us, a reminder that we should not touch His Glory. We are meant to carry it, not to own it.

Such is the blessing of being in God's presence that a whole nation was provided for in the middle of desert lands while in the Glory. Their clothes did not wear out and their stomachs were not empty. It would cost billions of dollars in resources, if not more, to keep 2 million people clothed and fed in the desert for 40 years. But God was the One keeping them, and there is no lack in the Glory. *"So when they measured it by omers, he who gathered much had nothing over, and he who gathered little had no lack..."* (Exodus 16:18).

The blessings were great, and so were the judgments. I covered some of those judgments in the chapter "The Father's Ways." Nothing in this world compares to being in His presence. David understood this, and from that understanding

The Ark of the Covenant *Chapter 4*

these words proceeded, *"How lovely is Your tabernacle, O LORD of hosts! My soul longs, yes, even faints for the courts of the LORD; my heart and my flesh cry out for the living God"* (Psalm 84:1-2).

The Ministry That Remains

Even so, the glory that was on the Ark was founded upon a covenant that would actually pass away. It won't fully pass, however, until heaven and earth themselves pass away (Matthew 5:18); but it is growing old, becoming obsolete, and is getting ready to vanish (Hebrews 8:13). I write this with fear, almost trembling, yet this is what the word says. What is available to us now is a surpassing glory that is eternal--the same God, just a New Covenant. And this new covenant includes the Gentiles! Because He remains the same, we can actually get to know Him by reading and seeing how He interacted with Israel under the Old Covenant.

"But if the ministry of death, written and engraved on stones, was glorious, so that the children of Israel could not look steadily at the face of Moses because of the glory of his countenance, which glory was passing away, how will the ministry of the Spirit not be more glorious? For if the ministry of condemnation had glory, the ministry of righteousness exceeds much more in glory. For even what was made glorious

Life In His Presence

had no glory that excels. For if what is passing away was glorious, what remains is much more glorious."

2 Corinthians 3:7-11

"The ministry of death, written and engraved on stones" has a glory that is fading away. Moses' face did not continue to shine after his encounter with God; little by little the glory lifted. This was a sign that the old covenant would also pass. *"For on the one hand there is an annulling of the former commandment because of its weakness and unprofitableness, for the law made nothing perfect; on the other hand, there is the bringing in of a better hope, through which we draw near to God"* (Hebrews 7:18-19), which is *"...Christ in you, the hope of glory"* (Colossians 1:27).

When Jesus became High Priest, by the oath made by His Father, there was a change of law (Hebrews 7:12). Before Jesus became High Priest, there were many high priests because death kept them from continuing to be priests (Hebrews 7:23). *"But He, because He continues forever, has an unchangeable priesthood. Therefore He is also able to save to the uttermost those who come to God through Him, since He always lives to make intercession for them"* (Hebrews 7:24-25). His priesthood is unchanging, and His Glory is unfading, only increasing. The priests under the order of Aaron carried a glory that was fading. But the unfading Glory of Jesus is carried on earth by His priests and will be carried by saints for all eternity. *"Of the increase of His government and peace there will be no end..."* (Isaiah 9:7). Even now it is only increasing.

The Holy Spirit, the One who brings glory to the Father and the Son by taking of what belongs to them and declaring it to us (John 16:14-15), is the One who reveals Jesus to us. He was at first with the disciples but would actually dwell in them. He dwells in us as the Spirit of Christ that dwells in us. He dwells in us as priests. *"But you are a chosen generation, a royal priesthood, a holy nation, His own special people, that you may proclaim the praises of Him who called you out of darkness into His marvelous light"* (1 Peter 2:9). This is how He has chosen to make His name great on the earth (Malachi 1:11)--through a people who will host His presence. We are the people upon whom He wants His glory to dwell.

Life In His Presence

Chapter 5

Hunger: A Key to the Glory

"One thing I have desired of the Lord, that I will seek, that I may dwell in the House of the Lord all of the days of my life; to behold the beauty of the Lord and to meditate in His temple... When you said 'Seek My Face' my heart said to You, 'Your Face, Lord, I will seek.'"

Psalm 27:4,8

Do you know why David experienced the Glory? Why he was able to access things from another age? Because he wanted Him. He accessed things reserved from another age because of the currency he carried, because of the key he carried around with him. Hunger. He desired to dwell in the Glory and so he positioned his life in such a way that he would constantly have his gaze set on Beauty. God made a way for the Hungry, and those who hunger can go as fast and as far as they

Life In His Presence

want. When I realized this, I started asking God to give me "Want": a want to experience His presence, to receive the benefits that are in it, to carry those things to others, and that this "want" would be greater than any want that the world has to offer.

Hunger is the currency of Heaven. It is the key to receiving anything that is heavenly. In the Kingdom, the hungry get fed. Jesus said *"Ask, seek and knock" (Matthew 7:7). "If you being evil know how to give good gifts to your children, how much more will your Heavenly Father give the Holy Spirit to those who ask Him"* (Luke 11:13).

When we ask God, we don't ask Him as orphans, but as sons. If we can have confidence that our earthly parents would give us food and supply our needs, how much more should we possess that same confidence in the Father. If you had a son and he asked you for bread, would you give him a stone? If you can trust yourself to give good gifts to your children, how much more can you trust the Father.

Hunger for God is, as Wade Taylor calls it, a "satisfied dissatisfaction" that brings Life. Any earthly addiction is a perversion of a greater reality called Hunger, which can almost seem like a Hunger for God, though it is only momentary and eventually brings death. The fruit produced by Hunger is eternal. Each drink of His Love is an eternal satisfaction.

Hunger: A Key to the Glory *Chapter 5*

Hunger is a longing for something or for someone that we lack. Jesus said, *"When the bridegroom is gone, then they will fast"* (Matthew 9:15). Jesus knew that His disciples would long for His return after He left and would, therefore, fast. Fasting is an expression and a reminder of the hunger and the longing that is in our spirits for the return of Christ, of the longing to be with Him where He is, that is, in fullness.

Hunger comes with life. You can somewhat tell how alive you truly are by how hungry you are for the Lord. Dead things do not hunger. Our hunger is satisfied as well as increased as we continue to get closer to the Living One, the One who gives us Life.

"If you knew the gift of God and Who it is Who says to you 'Give me drink,' you would have asked Him and He would have given you living water."

John 4:10

Jesus so desires to fill the thirsty that He will permit them to taste of things that are reserved for another time. There are many examples of this in the Bible, so let me name a few: Jesus turns the water into wine, Jesus offers the Holy Spirit to a Samaritan woman before He died on the cross, the prophets prophesy with the spirit of Christ who was in them (1 Peter 1:11). Hebrews 6 speaks of believers who have *"tasted the*

Life In His Presence

good word of God, and the powers of the age to come." The word *taste* used in this scripture is not accidental but purposed. The reason they got to taste it is because they were hungry.

Mary, the mother of Jesus, came to Him at the feast in Cana informing Him that the wedding had run out of wine and expecting Him to do something about it. Jesus' response in John 2:4 was, *"Woman, what does your concern have to do with Me? My hour has not yet come."* Mary then tells the servants *"Whatever He says to you, do it."* God honored her request and honored her confidence that He would act on her behalf, and He made wine.

"But without faith it is impossible to please Him, for he who comes to God must believe that He is and that He is a rewarder of those who diligently seek Him"

Hebrews 11:6

"... let him ask in faith, with no doubting, for he who doubts is like a wave of the sea driven and tossed by the wind. For let not that man suppose that he will receive anything from the Lord"

James 1:6-7

Jesus laid down just one condition for the Samaritan woman at the well, which was that of knowing Him. He said *"If you knew the gift of God and who it is who says to you 'give me* *drink,' you would have asked Him <u>and</u> He would have given you living water"* (John 4:10). If she knew the gift of God, she would desire It. If she knew Him who said to her give me drink, she would also know His great desire to give the gift of God, giving her confidence to ask Him for living water. The desire and confidence would have incited a request that Jesus could/would not resist/refuse. There are things in the Spirit that are reserved for the hungry. If you want it, you can have it.

Hunger in the natural will drive people to do some of the most extreme acts just to be satisfied, the most violent acts to get the thing they need. Think of what hungry people will do to get what they need. They do what they must with one purpose, and that is to be filled, but they do it without any promise of satisfaction. When we hunger and thirst after righteousness, Jesus promised that we would be filled. So our violent pursuit after God is not in fear of there not being enough for us, but with confidence that anything we ask in His Name, the Father will give it to us. Jesus says that *"the Kingdom suffers (allows) violence, and the violent take it by force"* (Matthew 11:12).

Hunger Gives Us Access

The LORD rebukes Israel in Isaiah 64:7 because *"there is no one who calls on [His] name, who stirs himself to take hold of [God]."* He had just mentioned that He acts on behalf of those who wait for Him, yet there was not one who would position himself to seek the LORD. We can actually stir ourselves up to take hold of Him; we don't have to be passive about it, for He has given us access. We don't stir ourselves up trying to earn anything, but do so because it is already ours. We are not trying to gain anything for He has already given us everything that we need for life and godliness (2 Peter 1). But we stir ourselves, appropriating what has been freely given to us (1 Corinthians 2). God has made Himself available to us, but we have to take hold of Him. He won't always spoon-feed us.

There is a difference between "orphan striving" and "confident partaking." Orphans seek approval and access, sometimes trying to take what is not theirs or feeling they must be really good to earn it. But sons already own what they are taking hold of. I ask God for His presence, and I know He will show up. I also enter in with thanksgiving and praise, being confident that I can do so. If I feel as though there is a wall, I press in because I know that I have access because I am a son. I don't just give up and say, "Well, maybe next time." No! The Lord is the portion of my inheritance and my cup, He maintains my lot (Psalm 16). So if I'm not experiencing all of my inheritance, I take hold of it. I am also confident whether or not I feel something, when I come into His presence, I am not wasting my time but that the Lord is with me. I have confidence that, when I position myself to receive, I am receiving and that when I enter into His presence, I am in His presence.

Hunger: A Key to the Glory — Chapter 5

Hungering for the Glory, for the manifest presence of God, is not a passive thing but is very active. Hunger demands an expression and its expression demands a response. This is the right context for striving, what it's supposed to be. Hunger leaves no room for toleration of the "same old same old." Those who cry out here are those who are heard in eternity. This is the place where it is right to be wild, to go all out, to have a hunger and a thirst that human words cannot quench or satisfy. Some people will say that you need to calm down; others will say that you should let God do it... and so on. But Jesus' Kingdom allows violence. In this place there is a Psalm 42 desperation. Let's not slow down but press in to all that He has for us--let's press in to encounter.

Hunger is the key into places in God that we could not otherwise access. It was David's hunger and confidence in the Lord that allowed him to do what others were punished for doing. Saul was judged for sacrificing animals (1 Samuel 15:22-25), but David sacrifices animals in the midst of judgment so that the LORD will lift His hand that was heavy on Israel. *"And David built there an altar to the LORD, and offered burnt offerings and peace offerings, and called on the LORD; and He answered him from heaven by fire on the altar of burnt offering"* (1 Chronicles 21:13). Saul, in his selfish ambition and fear of man, was not allowed to sacrifice animals. On the other hand, King David, because of His desire for God,

Life In His Presence

his repentance, and his humility, was told by God to erect an altar for burnt offering. David also partook of the bread that was reserved for the priests (1 Samuel 21). This hunger for the gift of God, and the confidence of knowing Him gave David access for things that were meant for another time.

Motivations for Hunger

Blessed are those who hunger and thirst for righteousness, for they shall be filled.

Matthew 5:6

There are many things for which humans hunger, but there is one kind of hunger and one kind of thirst that the Bible promises will be filled--Spiritual Hunger. There is a promise connected with Spiritual Hunger: Satisfaction. The promise is that what is desired will be received. Spiritual Hunger is for righteousness. Hunger after righteousness is the kind of hunger that is filled. When we delight ourselves in the Lord, He gives us the desires of our heart (Psalm 37:4). Those desires that He places in us He will fulfill.

The two main motivations given to us to pursue the Lord wholeheartedly are His Worthiness and His Reward. Both of these are very important and are both extremely needed. He is Worthy, and He is Worth it. The latter of the two is often confused with greed and selfishness and people hesitate in their radical pursuit after God, but we must understand that the Lord loves rewards. He loves to reward His people, and He loves it when His people desire the reward that He has promised and prepared for them. Just read Hebrews 11, Matthew 6, and 1 Corinthians 2:9 that emphasize "looking to the reward" and that encourage us to follow in the same example of our Fathers of Faith.

It is righteous to expect rewards and it is unrighteous not to expect or desire them. God expects hunger from us and is not ashamed to be called the God of those who desire. *"But now they desire a better, that is, a heavenly country. Therefore God is not ashamed to be called their God, for He has prepared a city for them"* (Hebrews 11:16).

Why is it righteous to desire? Because God is a rewarder; because where your treasure lies, there your heart will also lie (Matthew 6:21). We glorify the Lord when we desire and He fulfills. If we didn't have hunger, He who is Satisfaction would not have anyone to satisfy. Over and over again the scriptures exhort us to desire. *"But without faith it is impossible to please Him, for He who comes to God must believe that He is, and that He is a rewarder of those who diligently seek Him"* (Hebrews 11:6). Wow! So without expectant faith, God is not pleased with us? Without Faith that takes Him at His Word, and expects a reward, He is not pleased with us? Without Faith that believes that He is Worthy and that He is a rewarder?

Life In His Presence

So many of man's desires have been corrupted through the flesh, especially the desire for rewards, that people have become afraid to desire. They associate desire with sin and selfishness. But this is not so when He is our Reward, *"the Portion of our inheritance and our cup"* (Psalm 16:5). There is nothing wrong, and everything is right, in desiring what He has to offer, so be released and desire the reward. Be like Moses, *"Esteeming the reproach of Christ greater riches than the treasures in Egypt for he looked to the Reward"* (Hebrews 11:26).

Hunger for God always esteems the eternal above the temporal. Moses was motivated by a reward greater than what Egypt had to offer. Hunger and thirst that beckon eternal satisfaction is the key to wholeheartedness, the key to having a heart that is fully surrendered to God.

"The eyes of all look expectantly to You, and You give them their food in due season. You open Your hand and satisfy the desire of every living thing."

Psalm 145:15-16

Living things are those things that hunger. This is a main difference between a man and a stone, or a man and a dead body. The one that is alive hungers, but the one that is not alive is already satisfied and does not hunger. Hunger is a sign of life, and that is why He satisfies the desire of every living thing.

I have focused on the latter of the two motivations so far because it is the one that has been muddled so much. But we also need a revelation of how worthy He is. He is worthy because He created us. He is worthy because He delivered us. He is worthy because He loved us. He is worthy because He forgave us. He is worthy because He justified us. He is worthy because He chose us. He is worthy because… He is worthy because He is God, because He Is.

This is why we were created, to be amazed by His Beauty, and to desire to encounter Him. We were created to bring Him Glory. He wants somebody to whom He can reveal His Mercy and, when He does, He wants somebody who can praise Him because He is Mercy. He longs for someone to whom He can reveal His Worth and, when He does, He longs for someone who would forsake all earthly treasures for His treasures. His desire is to have someone to whom He can show that He is LOVE, and, when He does, He desires someone who can praise Him because He is Love.

Therefore, our success is in noticing His splendor and majesty and then responding to it when He reveals it to us. If you won't praise Him because you cannot feel it, then praise Him in Faith because He is Worthy!

There should be a desire in our hearts to see Him Glorified on the Earth. When someone is worthy, it is natural to

Life In His Presence

desire that they be honored and recognized for what they are worthy of. God is Worthy! And it is therefore rightly our desire to honor Him and our desire to see Him lifted High. We can be Hungry for His Glory, for Him to receive all Glory.

Both of these motivations are intermingled and really complement each other. Paul writes, *"Eagerly desire the greater gifts and I will show you a more excellent way"* (1 Corinthians 12:31), the way of Love. The reward He gives us brings Him Glory.

Revelation Produces Hunger

These ought to be overdriving motivations in our lives; but in order to walk in them, we need revelation of His Majesty and His Holiness. We cannot respond to what we have not encountered. But every believer has had an encounter, every person has somehow received faith or else he wouldn't be a believer. Therefore there is already a level of desire in every believer, but we need to turn it into an action. The only way to walk in that desire is to indulge in it, to seek the Lord. Whatever desire you invest into will be the one that will increase in your heart.

When we desire Him, we seek Him; when we seek Him, we find Him; when we find Him, we desire Him. We go higher and higher, deeper and deeper, from glory to Glory. He deserves our affections and our attention. Revelation produces desire, desire causes seeking, seeking engages encounter, and encounter releases revelation—and the cycle continues.

It is impossible to have hunger apart from having vision. You cannot long for something of which you have never tasted to some degree. Without a taste of His promise, we would be ignorant and would lack desire. People use the expression, "Ignorance is bliss"; I say, "Ignorance is ignorant." Ignorance keeps you from attaining what is available, from pressing for the upward call of God in Christ. The psalmist says, *"Oh, taste and see that the LORD is good; blessed is the man who trusts in Him"* (Psalm 34:8). The Lord likes to make sure that we know that He has something good in store for us and will often give us a taste so that we want more. That taste will give us vision, perseverance, and purpose to continue in a certain direction to attain the fullness of what we only tasted.

Jesus had a taste of the joy set before Him and therefore endured the cross and despised the shame (Hebrews 12:2). Abraham had a taste of the Heavenly City and did not settle for a city that he could build for himself (Hebrews 11:8-10). Moses had a taste of the riches of Christ and then forsook the riches of Egypt, leaving Egypt as seeing Him who is invisible (Hebrews 11:26-27). They had tasted and seen and then put their trust in God. Revelation produces desire.

When we have understanding about what God intends to do in us, through us, and for us, we can then place our hope in

Life In His Presence

the Lord to bring those things to pass. This kind of hunger and thirst positions us to be filled. Paul prayed for the Ephesians, *"That the God of our Lord Jesus Christ, the Father of Glory, may give to you the spirit of Wisdom and Revelation in the knowledge of Him, the eyes of your understanding being enlightened; that you may know what is the hope of His calling, what are the riches of the glory of His inheritance in the saints and what is the exceeding greatness of His power toward us who believe..."* (Ephesians 1:17-19).

We need to begin dreaming God-dreams once again. Dreams unto the Glory of God, that we could never accomplish on our own. Dreams for encounter with God that are rooted in revelation given by the Father. Dreams of preaching the Gospel to millions, with signs and wonders following. Dreams of turning whole nations to the Lord. Dreams of supernatural travail for hours or days that birth souls across the nations. Dreams of being visited by Jesus in trance visions. Dreams to see the Glory manifested in a cloud. Dreams of tangibly encountering God. I am not saying that <u>we</u> bring those dreams to pass; but when we position ourselves before the Lord, we will see <u>Him</u> bring them to pass. I have dreamed of experiencing many things in God. As I have positioned myself in His presence, the Lord has brought forth those kinds of encounters.

"Hope deferred makes the heart sick, but desire fulfilled is a tree of life" (Proverbs 13:12). When we put our hope in the Lord, we will not be disappointed. *"Behold, I lay in Zion a chief cornerstone, elect, precious, and he who believes (or trusts) on Him will by no means be put to shame"* (1 Peter 2:6). If our hope is not in Him, we will often experience heart sickness in our desire for good and even heavenly things..

I want to encourage you, in all your desiring, to desire the Lord. He may not do things the way that you are expecting, the way you are hoping, but know that He is doing something. A pitfall in desire is often desiring good things with a plan in mind on how they will come to pass. Let God be God. Dream big and let Him determine how to bring your dream to fruition. Let your dreams be so big that you cannot bring them to pass, and don't try to make it happen, Remember that He is able *"to do exceeding abundantly above all that we ask or think"* (Ephesians 3:20).

Keep asking Him, keep seeking Him, keep knocking at His door. Do not stop dreaming. Do not stop desiring. Do not be afraid. He will not leave you hanging. He is your Shepherd and you shall not want (Psalm 23). Those who fear Him, those who trust in Him, lack no good thing (Psalm 34). Put your trust in Him and keep asking.

Life In His Presence

Hindrances to Hunger

The kisses of His word equip us to have the hunger needed so that we can be filled. It is those revelations of His beauty, those kisses of His word, that in turn become invitations for Hunger. If that place of hunger is being satisfied by something else, you have greatly limited yourself. You can have as much as you want; but if you don't want it, God will find somebody else that does. I used to constantly ask God to send the fire of His Spirit so that anything that stands in the way may be removed. I didn't want anything to rob me of the fullness.

One of the greatest hindrances to hunger is legitimate pleasure, though most of our "legitimate pleasures" are not legitimate at all. I must say that anything that tolerates sin and that we ourselves tolerate is not legitimate. They are sin, and sin is definitely a hindrance. Though legitimate pleasures are not wrong, they sometimes actually get in the way of what God wants to do in our life. The Laodicean church was so dulled by these that Jesus said He would spew them out of His mouth. Television can be a legitimate pleasure but it will often take up so much of that limited resource called time and that currency called Hunger that we don't have much left for God.

The Lord had me go through a season of giving up many legitimate, as well as illegitimate, pleasures. I stopped watching TV for the most part, maybe watching a movie once every two or three months. I stopped playing video and computer games. I found that surfing the internet and Facebook expended too much of my limited time. For that season of my life, I chose to lay aside all these hindrances so that I could increasingly walk in the power of God. I laid them down, not because they were all sin, but so that I could enter into encounter with God.

This is not legalism--it is Desire. You spend more time with whatever you enjoy most. Time is a resource, and we can use it for that which brings us the most pleasure. But what brings us the most pleasure? *"My people are destroyed for lack of knowledge"* (Hosea 4:6). If we don't know that God is most pleasurable, then we will use our resources on others.

In that season, I began to encounter God as I had never before. I stumbled into His presence one time as I was worshipping Him. I did not plan it or even expect it, but He surprised me. I was just sitting in front of my parents' computer and decided to turn on some worship music that was saved in the music program in the computer. As I started worshipping the Lord, He met me, gave me a taste, and I was never able to go back. From that time on I knew, because I had tasted, that I had access into His presence and that it was very sweet and enjoyable.

I wanted to walk in the power of God, and I knew that I couldn't walk in fullness with compromise in my heart, so I lay down a lot of things. I had no idea what awaited me. In that season of encounter I reached the point where I would simply

Life In His Presence

close my eyes, quietly say "Hallelujah" or another expression of worship, and His presence would fill my being. I would come home from school and run into my room to worship God. It became my favorite part of the day.

I believe the reason why many don't encounter Him frequently and deeply is because we don't give Him room in our cluttered lives. Hunger begets hunger. When you say "Yes" to His call, when you participate in His invitation, then more hunger will be given. The more you give yourself to something that is enjoyable the more you begin to enjoy it. That is how we were made. You don't come to enjoy prayer by playing basketball; you come to enjoy it by praying and then by encountering the Beautiful One.

"Do not love the world or the things in the world. If anyone loves the world, the love of the Father is not in him. For all that is in the world--the lust of the flesh, the lust of the eyes, and the pride of life--is not of the Father but is of the world."

1 John 2:15-16

Daily extended engagement in media (TV, video games, Facebook, etc.) can keep you from entering into the "more" that is available to you, and I believe your encounter with the Lord will be limited. I'm not saying you are in sin, but I do believe that this can be a strong hindrance. There is a commandment in the scriptures that says, "Thou shall not check Facebook more than twice a day" (2 Sebastian 5:16)... Just kidding. But again, I do believe these things can be a hindrance to hunger for God. These can be some of the thorns Jesus talks about that hinder our growth in the knowledge of God. *"Now these are the ones sown among thorns; they are the ones who hear the word, and the cares of this world, the deceitfulness of riches, and the <u>desires for other things</u> entering in choke the word, and it becomes unfruitful"* (Mark 4:18-19).

I focus a lot on media because that's where a lot of my focus went instead of the Lord. I still don't these things perfectly, but I seek to surrender more and more of my time to Him in order to go higher and higher with Him. There are many other things that distract us from His Beauty: unhealthy relationships, worry, anxious thoughts, lusts, and things that fill our minds and use up much our time. These things will distract us from using that resource of time to gaze on Beauty.

I want to challenge any who daily participate in these things that are potential distractions or areas where the Holy Spirit has been tugging at your heart. Take a 21-day media fast, purpose to set aside an hour daily to worship Him, even outside of the church services, and see what happens. After those 21 days, see if you notice anything different when you begin doing these things again. Many of you may notice a dulling in your heart as you participate in these potential distractions from the

Life In His Presence

Beauty of Holiness. If you do, then you have to evaluate what is a priority in your life: His presence or temporary entertainment? Are you going to hell if you do these things? NO!! That's not what I'm saying at all--but there is so much more available, and I want us all to take hold of it and find the greater pleasure.

Ho! Everyone who thirsts, come to the waters; and you who have no money, come, buy and eat. Yes, come, buy wine and milk without money and without price. Why do you spend money for what is not bread, and your wages for what does not satisfy? Listen carefully to Me, and eat what is good, and let your soul delight itself in abundance.

Isaiah 55:1-2

The Lord is not interested in what we have to offer, but in the need that we present to Him. It doesn't cost us anything-- He paid the price--but He will not give to those who do not want it. He will not satisfy those who have already filled themselves with things that do not satisfy. Not because He is mean, but because there is no room. The Lord is saying, "Repent, come to me, I will satisfy." And if we will turn to Him, emptying ourselves from all other lovers, He will satisfy. We have to trust Him. We have nothing to offer, just a need to present.

Counting the Cost

Carrying the Glory is a great privilege but it does not come without a price. The only way that we can persevere and endure this race is by letting go of everything that hinders and looking unto the reward, Jesus. Jesus understood that His reward would cost Him His life and so *"for the joy set before Him, He endured the Cross, despising the shame"* (Hebrews 12:2). We have to understand both the cost and the reward in order to persevere and to endure. The cost is ..., well, everything. He is an all-consuming Fire, and His presence is what we long to carry. He gave all of His life, and He expects no less from us.

In Galatians Paul put it this way, *"It is no longer I who live, but Christ lives in me, and the life that I now live in the flesh I live by faith in the Son of God, Who loved me and gave himself for me"* (Galatians 2:20). In Philippians he puts it this way, *"I count all things loss for the excellence of the knowledge of Christ Jesus my Lord, for whom I have suffered the loss of all things, and count them as rubbish, that I may gain Christ...That I may know Him and the power of His resurrection, and the fellowship of His suffering, being conformed to His death, if, by any means, I may attain to the resurrection from the dead"* (Philippians 3:8,10).

We will not receive in this age the pinnacle of the reward for which we are presently counting the cost, yet what

Life In His Presence

we get to taste of the reward here in this age makes it worth counting and paying the cost in the present. Paul gives us a glimpse into the pinnacle of what we are running this race for later in the third chapter of Philippians. Christ will *"transform our lowly body that it may be conformed to His glorious body, according to the working by which He is able even to subdue all things to Himself"* (Philippians 3:21).

Those who have carried this treasure in earthen vessels were literally pressed on every side by persecutions. They experienced the same glory that was manifested on the cross, that of laying down their lives for friends and even enemies. Jesus said in John 15 that we should abide in the vine and then in verse 20, *"...a servant is not greater than his Master. If they persecuted Me, they will also persecute you."*

Paul wrote in 2 Corinthians 4:10, *"Always carrying about in the body the dying of the Lord Jesus, that the life of Jesus also may be manifested in our body."* I believe that persecution is promised to those who abide in the vine, to those who carry the presence of God. This does not sound very exciting, but we have this assurance in 2 Corinthians 4:17, *"For our light affliction, which is but for a moment, is working for us a far more exceeding and eternal weight of glory."* We carry the dying of the Lord Jesus in our bodies through persecution, but we also carry the life of Jesus who is manifested in our bodies.

Most important to counting the cost is the realization that the reward itself is of greater value than the cost. The reward is more valuable than anything we can give up or suffer, and yet it has been made available to us on the condition that we lay down everything for God. The reward is not just something in the future but it is available now. Eternal life does not start when our natural body dies and we get a resurrected body; it begins when our spirits receive the Breath of God. Presently there is a great reward--it is called intimacy, knowing Jesus, which is eternal life (John 17:3). We can now experience and partake of eternal life and of its benefits.

A major part of the cost is the laying down of unrighteous mindsets and habits. I believe that Philippians 3 touches best on what counting the cost really looks like and why we would want to count it. "In view of the surpassing greatness of knowing Christ Jesus...count all things as loss" (Paraphrase). Our unrighteousness and our own righteousness are part of the things that we are to count as loss, all for the greater value of knowing Jesus.

There are sure benefits to being in the presence of God, to having the manifest presence wherever you are. Of course, those benefits are only in the context of a broken and contrite heart (Isaiah 66). Where pride and sin abide, the manifest presence of God brings judgment. That is why the blessing Jesus brings to the nations is the gift of repentance.

Life In His Presence

"Repent therefore and be converted, that your sins may be blotted out, so that times of refreshing may come from the presence of the Lord ... He said to Abraham, 'and in your seed all the nations of the earth shall be blessed.' <u>To you first</u>*, God, having raised up His Servant Jesus,* <u>sent him to bless you, in turning away every one of you from your iniquities</u>*."*

Acts 3:19,25b-26

1 Corinthians 3:16-17 points out that we, as a body, are the temple of the Holy Spirit. Verse 17 says, *"If anyone defiles the temple of God, God will destroy him. For the temple of God is holy, which temple you are."* They were defiling the temple through their disunity, by slandering one another and picking sides rather than being in one accord.

1 Corinthians 6:17-20 points out that our bodies are temples of the Holy Spirit: *"But he who is joined to the Lord is one spirit with Him. Flee sexual immorality. Every sin that a man does is outside the body, but he who commits sexual immorality sins against his own body. Or do you not know that your body is the temple of the Holy Spirit who is in you, who you have from God, and you are not your own? For you were bought at a price; therefore, glorify God in your body and in your spirit, which are God's."* By their impurity they were keeping themselves from walking as one with the Spirit of God. We too must be pure if we are to be one with the Holy Spirit.

The Glory will not abide in sin and sin certainly will not abide in the Glory. We can choose which of these two we will be in agreement with. If we agree with Glory, sin will not be able to abide in us but will be judged (Galatians 5, Romans 8). If we agree with sin, being unrepentant, then we will separate ourselves from the presence of God for *"God resists the proud, but gives grace to the humble"* (James 4:6). This scripture is in context of the indwelling Spirit and drawing near to God. We draw near to God in repentance, as we turn to Him and as we acknowledge our need for Him.

This ministry of the Spirit, whose glory remains and increases, unlike the ministry of death, is the ministry of reconciliation. It is the ministry of reconciling men to God through the revelation of Jesus Christ. This is impossible without repentance, without turning. It is as we turn and as others turn that the veil is lifted and we may behold the Glory of the Lord and thereby be transformed into His likeness from glory to Glory.

ASK: Expression of Hunger

"If you being evil know how to give good gifts to your children, how much more will your Heavenly Father give the Holy Spirit to those who ask Him."

Luke 11:13

Life In His Presence

My life in the Lord has been marked by this expression of ASKing God. ASK: Ask, Seek, and Knock (Matthew 7:7). I heard someone use this acrostic once and have kept it ever since, and I believe that these three words are the essential expression of Hunger. The Lord doesn't want us just to desire, but He wants us to express our desire to Him--He made us for relationship. These are such important expressions and there is a lot to cover here, but we will mainly focus on the first expression, "Ask."

Whenever the Lord got hold of my heart, He would always do it by giving me Hunger, doing things that would make me desire Him more. The first time I remember His doing this was when I was about 4 years old. My oldest brother had gone up to the altar at church that Sunday morning. As they prayed for him, the power of God came on him and he fell to the floor. While he was on the floor, the Lord spoke to him and told him that He was going to use him in the ministry. That day he told our family what his experience had been and that the Lord had spoken to him.

When I heard of his experience with the Lord, there was a holy jealousy that was stirred in my heart. I decided that I also wanted to experience God in this way, that I wanted to hear His voice. From that day on I began to ask the Lord continually to speak to me. For some time I asked Him various times a day to speak to me. As time passed, I would ask Him whenever it came to my mind. The Lord used my brother's experience to draw me near to Himself. I don't know about you, but whenever I hear a story of what God is doing in someone else or in a certain place, desire is stirred in my heart and I find myself longing for Him to touch me in a similar way.

Whenever we experience any level of desire for the Kingdom of God and His Righteousness, it is our responsibility to steward it. That Hunger is a gift from the Lord, even an empowering, a key and a guarantee of being filled. It is an empowering to pursue the Lord, and it guarantees that you will be filled by Him. When Jesus said in Matthew 7, "Ask, seek and knock," this was not a one-time thing, but a continual expression. The Greek there more correctly translated would be this: "Asking and you shall receive, seeking and you will find, knocking and the door will be opened to you" (Matthew 7:7). The way that we steward Hunger is by ASKing. This is how you turn desire into an action.

Many people have experienced this desire but did not know that they had access to Him who is Desire Fulfilled and, therefore, did not press in to obtain what they desired. They did not think to ask for something they did not believe they would receive. They believed, not that God <u>couldn't</u> give it to them but that He <u>wouldn't</u>. Others didn't even consider that as a possibility. Still others experienced hope deferred and grew hardened, as a means to protect themselves. They didn't want to

Life In His Presence

ask because they didn't want to go through the pain of believing and not seeing.

Before I realized what was available to me, I did not have any reason to fast, to pray, or to long. But once the Lord showed me what was available, longing was awakened in my heart. One time when I was ten, I thought about the dynamic ministry of a certain man of God. God uses him to preach the gospel to thousands with signs and wonders following his ministry. I thought to myself, "That would be cool if I could do something like that." When I was six-years-old the extent of my dreaming was to have a family, a really good paying job, and $1,000. I only dreamed of things that I felt I could do. The Lord responded to my thoughts with another thought that I immediately recognized as God's speaking to me. He said, "Why not?" My brain then began to swirl as I realized that God actually wanted to use me. I said, "Really!! Wow!" Faith came by hearing, and hearing by His Word! (Romans 10:17).

This encounter with the Lord was actually the answer to 6 years of ASKing to hear His voice. I had expected it to be a booming voice, a thundering of God's voice speaking to me, and I definitely expected it sooner than later. But it came about 6 years later and it came as a whisper, not as a shout. The answer and filling of one desire was the beginning of more desire. He is still answering that prayer to hear His voice and has not stopped.

Hunger: A Key to the Glory   *Chapter 5*

When I found out that the gifts of the Spirit were available to me, that I could actually desire them (1 Corinthians 12:31), I began to ASK constantly for the Holy Spirit. I began to ASK God for God, and He could not resist but to give Himself to me. I spent 6 months asking for the gift of tongues before I actually received it; I would ask on a nearly daily basis for it, if not more.

"You have not because you ask not, and when you do ask, you ask amiss" (James 4:3). The Lord had me asking primarily for His presence and spiritual blessings, i.e., anything that involved Him. He answered those prayers and manifested in His own time and in His own way.

I've asked the Lord for many things, even to be transported by the Spirit as Phillip was in Acts 8. The Lord answered this prayer one day when I least expected it and it freaked me out, as well as my friend who was driving. We were traveling north on Route 1 and saw what seemed like a shooting star the size of a golf ball or baseball 500 feet in the air. The next thing we knew we appeared on another road. The name of that other road is "Lafayette," which actually means faith. I've asked God for the gift of healing and have witnessed hundreds of people healed of diverse things.

I've asked for an ability to write and express revelation and this book in your hands is a first-fruits. James said that when they did ask they asked amiss. A key to remember in

Life In His Presence

asking is to ask for things that are according to His will. If they bring Glory to His Name, then ASK.

I share these testimonies to encourage you, though I'm afraid I cannot give you an exact formula to replicate these events. The Bible says, however, to "ASK." Desire, press in, push past every weight, and then wait on the Lord to act. Things that I have asked for have not always come when I expected them, or how I expected them, but He is always Faithful. Don't be afraid to desire, to dream again, to trust the Lord, and don't grow weary in waiting on Him. *"For since the beginning of the world men have not heard nor perceived by the ear, nor has the eye seen any God besides You, Who acts for the one who waits for Him"* (Isaiah 64:4).

I have seen the Lord give me many things that I have asked for, and it is no wonder that He does since He promised that He would give the Holy Spirit to those, who as children, ask the Father. Do you know of the perseverance of a child? They will often ask and keep on asking until they get what they want. We were wired to desire and to be fulfilled. A child believes that his earthly father has the resources and more to give him the toy that He wants, even if his father really doesn't; believing this, he asks, even though that toy has not been given him or even promised to him.

On the other hand, our heavenly Father does have all the resources and has already given us every spiritual blessing in the Heavenly places (Ephesians 1:3). Notice here I am talking about asking, not begging. We don't have to convince Him; He is already convinced, has already made up His mind, and has already given it to you. *"His divine power has given to us all things that pertain to life and godliness, through the knowledge of Him who called us by Glory and virtue"* (2 Peter 1:3).

David's longing for the courts of the LORD gave him access to them. He had tasted and seen, and he then decided that he wanted some more. If you find that you lack this key to His presence--Hunger--ask Him for it. He is ready to give it to us. He longs for us to be near to Him, for us to know Him.

"How lovely is Your tabernacle, O LORD of hosts! My soul longs, yes, even faints for the courts of the LORD; my heart and my flesh cry out for the living God."

Psalm 84:1-2

Life In His Presence

Chapter 6

The Glory of Intercession: Seated in Heavenly Places

Presently Jesus is positioned in what we call the Session at the right hand of the Majesty on high. The word "session" is derived from a Latin word, *sedere*, which means "to sit." Two times in the book of Hebrews, Psalm 110 is quoted: *"Sit at my right hand, till I make Your enemies Your footstool"* (Hebrews 1:13; 10:13) and three times it is mentioned that Jesus is seated at the right hand of the Majesty in the Heavens (Hebrews 1:4; 8:1; 10:12). This is an important position that He is in, and it is important that we understand where He is.

Jesus gained this position as He was in complete submission to the Father. Hebrews 5:4 says that *"Christ did not glorify Himself to become High Priest, but it was He who said to Him: 'You are My Son; today I have begotten You.'"* He humbled Himself to the point of death on a cross. *"Therefore God also has highly exalted Him and given Him the name which is above every name, that at the Name of Jesus every*

Life In His Presence

knee should bow, of those in heaven and of those on earth, and of those under the earth, and that every tongue should confess that Jesus Christ is Lord, to the glory of God the Father" (Philippians 2:8-11).

The way Ephesians puts it is that God worked His mighty power in raising Jesus from the dead *"and seated Him at His right hand in the heavenly places, far above all principality and power and might and dominion, and every name that is named, not only in this age but also in that which is to come. And He put all things under His feet, and gave Him to be head over all things to the church, which is His body, the fullness of Him who fills all in all"* (Ephesians 1:19-23).

He has been seated above every power, principality, name, throne, etc. He is at the right hand of the Father, waiting until His enemies are made His footstool. He is sitting because He is completely assured of His inheritance and reward. He has overcome the world and is presently waiting for His Father to make His enemies His footstool, for the time He comes back to execute Justice.

His rule does not come from a place of struggling and trying really hard, but from a place of peace and complete confidence. He is at the right hand of the Father and He knows that anything He asks He will receive. He always lives to make intercession.

The apostle's prayer in Acts 4 is interesting when we see

it in this light. They did not ask Jesus to come down and take care of things because they understood that He has all Authority. They simply asked, *"Stretch out Your hand."* There is a day coming when He Himself will execute justice on the earth. He will split the skies, come down, and judge the nations. Psalm 2 says that He will dash nations to pieces. However, while He is in Session, all He has to do is stretch out His hand, and whatever He purposes, in the act of stretching out His hand, will come to pass.

His Father has sworn; therefore, He has nothing to worry about. *"The LORD has sworn and will not relent, 'You are a priest forever according to the order of Melchizedek'"* (Psalm 110:4). He was given this position by His Father because He died. *"...When He came into the world, He said: 'Sacrifice and offering You have not desired, but a body You have prepared for Me'"* (Hebrews 10:5). When He came to the earth, He was given a prepared body to offer as a sacrifice. Hebrews 10:10 says, *"By that will we have been sanctified through the offering of the body of Jesus Christ once for all."* His work is complete; now He just has to wait.

Seated with Christ

Everything we do ought to be done from the manifest presence of God. Since we have access, why not take full advantage of what has been made available to us. Christ raised us up and made us to sit together with Him in the heavenly places (Ephesians 2:6). Because of this, the ministry of intercession is not based on our strengths or on how well we can articulate a prayer. It is based on the authority of Christ as we enter into agreement, as we are seated, with Him in Heavenly places.

That we are seated with Him demonstrates that we are in agreement with Him. We sit with Him because we are in agreement. So when He says "Father, I desire...," we say "Amen!" I believe David experienced a taste of this reality and recorded it in Psalm 110: *"The LORD said to my Lord, 'Sit at My right hand, till I make Your enemies Your footstool.'"* Hearing the counsels of the LORD, he had the opportunity to step into agreement with them and even declare them to all who would ever read the Psalms. Intercession is when we "Enter-Session" with Him.

The position of sitting is a position of authority. It is a position of confidence. And that is what Jesus is doing--He is sitting at the right hand of the Majesty in the heavens. He is at the right hand of the Father, which is the position from which He ever lives to make intercession for us. He has invited us into that same ministry of intercession. We come to the Father not as widows and orphans but as the Bride and as sons and as coheirs with Christ. The Father said to the Son, *"Ask of Me and I will give You the nations as Your inheritance"* (Psalm 2:8). Jesus made us coheirs, so we ask the Father with boldness and confidence for the nations. We ask Him for what He already wants to give His Son; we "Enter-Session."

Intercession is when one party speaks on another's behalf. This can be seen both when a person prays for a group or nation, speaking to God on their behalf, or when a person prophesies over a nation, speaking to the people on behalf of God. Both are necessary. Jesus did both from a heavenly position. In speaking with Nicodemus, He claimed that He was both in Heaven and there standing with Nicodemus on earth (John 3). Likewise He prayed, *"Father, I desire that they also whom You gave Me may be with Me where I am, that they may behold My glory which You have given Me..."* (John 17:24). He did not pray, "that they would be with me where I'm going," but, *"that they may be with Me <u>where I am</u>"* (John 17:24).

I believe Psalms 2 and 110 are an insight into the Session of Jesus Christ, of Him who sits at the right hand of the Majesty on high, as well as an insight into His Second Coming. I believe they also give insight into just how He manifests His dominion on the earth as He sits in Heaven. He manifests His dominion on earth through those who ask and through those who walk in demonstration of the Spirit and of power--through intercessors. Both of these are acts of Intercession. Remember, intercession is not just one-sided; intercession involves both parties. When God is the one speaking, or responding, things

Life In His Presence

tend to be more explosive. The Apostles quote Psalm 2 when they ask God to give them boldness by stretching out His hand to heal and by performing signs and wonders through the name of Jesus. They took an eschatological passage having to do with God judging kings and nations and applied it to God giving them boldness by healing the sick. And God responded <u>to</u> them, and responded <u>through</u> them.

Psalm 110:3 says, *"Your people shall be volunteers in the day of Your power; in the beauties of holiness..."* It will be because of His Beauty and Power that His people will volunteer freely. I believe part of the partnership here is beholding His beauty and worshipping Him. And this is how He manifests His dominion on earth while sitting in Heaven. He lets us see His Glory, that what we have seen, we may display. These verses will be fulfilled fully in the end, though I believe part of this fulfillment is through lovers seeing His Beauty and being empowered to demonstrate His Power.

Humility: The Glory of Heaven

"If then you were raised with Christ, seek those things which are above, where Christ is, sitting at the right hand of God. Set your mind on things above, not on things on the earth. For you died, and your life is hidden with Christ in God."

Colossians 3:1-3

The Glory of Intercession   *Chapter 6*

We participate with Christ's ministry of intercession by setting our minds on things above, *"in the beauties of holiness"* (Psalm 110:3). And we enter into that ministry the same way that He did. He humbled Himself to the point of death, and when we join Him in His death, we likewise join Him in His life. He ever lives to make intercession.

Jesus received this position of authority from the Father by humbling Himself. We also get to enter into that Glory through humility. Without it, we cannot function in that authority. Things in the Kingdom work significantly different than in the kingdoms of this world. Do you want to be a leader and have a lasting legacy? Get on your knees and exalt the God of Israel and prefer others above yourself. Jesus said it this way, *"But he who is greatest among you shall be your servant"* (Matthew 23:11).

Jesus died a death that was not His to die, and paid the price for evil that He had not committed. The great Glory, the outstanding nature, the ways of Jesus, is that He, being Great, lowered Himself. That which is not seen on earth He brought with Him from the heart of His Father. What worldly king would stoop down to serve his subjects, much less to serve his enemies? Jesus expressed qualities that are foreign to the sinful, fallen nature. That is what makes Him *"outstanding among ten thousand"* (Song of Songs 5:10b).

Life In His Presence

Colossians 3 says that we *"were raised with Christ."* What was He raised from, and what were we raised from with Him? We were raised from death, from separation with God. We presently experience this reality to a limited degree, for it is hidden. We will experience it more fully or more manifest as Colossians 3:4 says, *"When Christ who is our life appears, then you also will appear with Him in glory."* We are hidden in Christ, who is hidden in God, but when He appears, we will likewise appear. This ministry of intercession is not a spotlight ministry but it is a ministry that in this age is hidden. Not many will see it, and those who set their minds on the things of the earth cannot comprehend it.

The fact that it is not manifest here on earth does not take away from the authority and Glory that it carries in the heavens, nor does its being veiled take away from its governmental impact in the here-and-now. Jesus walked on the earth and withheld manifesting all of His Glory. This did not take away from who He is, and it did not take away from the glory that He carried. It just made it so that he whose eyes were set on earthly things could not recognize Him or understand the extent of His glory. Those who are fixed on appearance in this age miss what God is really doing. They miss the revelation that does not come from flesh and blood but from our Father in Heaven. The fact that it is not manifest here on earth does mean that our intercession will likely not be rewarded nor reputed by

The Glory of Intercession   *Chapter 6*

men in this age but rather disregarded and even despised by them.

Hindrances to Intercession

There are clashes between God's ways and our own that prove to be a hindrance to the heart posture for intercession. These differences are mostly rooted in the desire to make a difference by our own ability, rather than agreeing with God and letting Him make the impact. Prayer is not a matter of quantity but of quality, and that quality comes with agreement. It's not about how long, how loud, how sad, how convincing, how articulate, or even how theologically correct we pray. Someone can pray for five minutes and shift things in the Spirit simply because in that time they came into agreement with God. Not because they prayed really loud, or long enough, but because their genuine prayer was in agreement with God's will. Long, articulate prayers prayed loudly are simply *"vein repetitions"* when they are not genuine. Genuine does not mean that you feel every syllable you pray but more so that the purpose of your prayer, more than a religious duty, is to agree with the Father. If you don't mean what you pray, it is meaningless.

We don't have to sit around and try to figure out what God's will is or worry about whether we are praying His will or not. The Bible says that His will is that *"none should perish but that all come to repentance"* (2 Peter 2:9). He came to give life and life *"more abundantly"* (John 10:10). When He walked on the earth, Jesus healed all the sick who came to or who were brought to Him, as well as others that He just came to on His way. Pray those things that we see clearly in the scriptures are according to His will. *"Now this is the confidence that we have in Him, that if we ask anything according to His will, He hears us. And if we know that He hears us, whatever we ask, we know that we have the petitions that we have asked of Him"* (1 John 5:14-15).

God has invited us into confidence. *"Let us therefore come boldly to the throne of grace, that we may obtain mercy and find grace to help in time of need"* (Hebrews 4:16). We don't have to beg God for anything or even try to convince Him. Praying for ourselves is not selfish, nor is asking God for the very things He told us to ask Him for. Because we are His children, we can ask Him and not beg Him, for He already wants to move on our behalf.

This confidence is to be rooted in the finished work of the Cross and not on our own righteousness. We do not deserve anything from God. No matter how good we are, God is not indebted to us. He will not listen to me more than somebody else because I am more "righteous" than they. That arrogant standpoint is on a shaky foundation and is not in agreement with His Ways. The religious of Jesus' day thought like this,

The Glory of Intercession   *Chapter 6*

and Jesus said they would not be justified (Luke 18:10-14). There are no super Christians, only blood-bought saints. God will listen to us because the Blood of His Son covers us.

If our allegiance is divided, we will have a hard time in the place of prayer. Jesus said that no one can serve two masters (Matthew 6). When our affections are set on other things, the place of prayer can become a burdensome labor, boring and hard. *"Do not love the world or the things in the world. If anyone loves the world, the love of the Father is not in him. For all that is in the world--the lust of the flesh, the lust of the eyes, and the pride of life--is not of the Father but is of the world"* (1 John 2:15-16).

Sometimes we may not even notice or want to admit that our attention is set on other things than Jesus, but those idols must be cast down if we want to be in real agreement with the Father. God even said to Jeremiah that He would not listen to the cry of those whose allegiance with Him was divided in the day of their trouble.

One way that is not in agreement with His is unforgiveness. This way of the flesh is contrary to the work that He accomplished on the Cross; it is contrary to His Mercy and Patience. Jesus teaches His disciples how to pray in the Sermon on the Mount. He concludes His teaching on prayer by stating that if we do not forgive those who wrong us the Father will not forgive us. *"For if you do not forgive men their trespasses,*

Life In His Presence

neither will your Father forgive your trespasses" (Matthew 6:14). If we do not forgive, we do not step into God's forgiveness and rob ourselves of boldness with which to approach the Father.

If there is disunity and offense in our hearts, we will be crippled in corporate intercession. Agreement is essential in the place of prayer--agreement with God and with one another. It is no coincidence that Jesus speaks about corporate prayer in the middle of teaching about how to deal with offense. Matthew 18:15-17 speaks on how to deal with offense between brethren, and verses 18-20 speak about the power of agreement in the place of prayer. *"Assuredly, I say to you, whatever you bind on earth will be bound in heaven, and whatever you loose on earth will be loosed in heaven. Again I say to you that if two or three agree on earth concerning anything that they ask, it will be done for them by My Father in heaven. For where two or three are gathered together in My name, I am there in the midst."*

Jesus said that we should first reconcile with our brethren before offering our gifts at the altar. Before engaging in an act of worship and communion with God, our hearts need to be free from offense. If you have ever tried to pray while you are mad at somebody, you may have already noticed that most of your focus went towards that individual and that situation rather than towards God. Unfortunately, there are times when we are unable to reconcile or communicate with a person.

Should we then not pray until we speak with the individual and reconcile? No. We need to forgive them in our hearts if they have wronged us, and we need to set in our hearts to speak with the individual and follow through with the decision. Feeling hurt is not wrong, but we should not hold offense against the individual who has hurt us.

The power of life and death is in the tongue (Proverbs 18:21) and we need to watch, therefore, what we agree with. The Lord looks at the heart. He will know if your feelings towards a person are bad. However, when you come into agreement with those emotions or with somebody else's and express them audibly, you have just pulled a trigger in the Spirit. There is power in the tongue and there is power in agreement. We will eat the fruit of our tongue, whether Life or Death (Proverbs 18:21). Do not side with the enemy or with the flesh on this matter but rather repent. Gossip ought not to have a place in the mouth or heart of a believer. If you have engaged in such activity, repent and bless those you have spoken against.

Jesus gives us a prescription on how to deal with our enemies and those who persecute us: Bless them! *"But I say to you, love your enemies, bless those who curse you, do good to those who hate you, and pray for those who spitefully use you and persecute you, that you may be sons of your Father in heaven; for He makes His sun rise on the evil and on the good, and sends rain on the just and on the unjust"* (Matthew 5:44-

45). By blessing those who curse us, we come into agreement with our Father in Heaven.

The Offense of Intercession

There is a great misunderstanding in the human mind of anything that God does. He said *"Your thoughts are not my thoughts nor are your ways My Ways"* (Isaiah 55:8). The way He moves is offensive to the carnal mind. He told many of His disciples that they had to eat His flesh and drink His blood; their response was to walk away (John 6:53-66). The ones that stayed with Him were also offended in their minds but remained because they understood that He alone had the words of Life.

In every revival and move of the Spirit somebody has been offended about something. Because intercession also is a moving of the Holy Spirit in believers, it is offensive. It is a moving within the human heart to agree with God's desires and to partner with Him by asking Him for the things that He is already longing to give. God is all-powerful and can do whatever He wants to do, but in His sovereignty He has decided that He won't do things without us. Jesus said that if we ask the Father in His Name, in Jesus' Name, the Father would give it to us. This moving of the Spirit is offensive to the un-renewed mind.

The Glory of Intercession   *Chapter 6*

Presently many are confused by the prayer movement or by people that like to pray a lot. There is much confusion and many things that are misunderstood. Questions arise such as: "Why the screaming or loudness?" "Is this Striving?" "Why do they look angry when they pray--isn't there supposed to be joy in the House of Prayer?" "What is this travail thing all about?" "24/7 prayer, is that balanced?" These are some of the questions that I have heard the most. At times they have been asked from a critical standpoint, though often times they are asked by those who have genuine concern or desire to understand.

People have asked me why some intercessors look angry when they pray. I recently thought about that question, and the Lord reminded me of a drummer I know who frowns when he plays the drums. He loves to play the drums and plays them very well, but his facial expression is that of frowning whenever he plays the drums. I don't think he does it on purpose and I know that he doesn't feel upset, but that's just the look he gets when he is focused on playing the drums. I probably have one of those "mean" faces sometimes when I intercede, but I'm not angry, just focused.

Outwardly that seems to contradict the joy that was promised in His house (Isaiah 57). The good news is that those fruits that God promised us are primarily spiritual realities and not appearance realities. The Lord has given me a lot of joy and it is often seen outwardly. When I'm interceding, my

Life In His Presence

appearance does not always seem joyful, but it is often times in that deep intercession that I experience one of my greatest enjoyments. People get upset at the appearance, and demons get upset at the power, leading to a perfect scenario for offense. I don't know if it's really that simple but maybe it truly is.

Some people get really excited when they pray and their voices rise with their excitement. Though there may be cause in different circumstances to ask people to keep their voices down, I personally don't see anything wrong with this excitement (perhaps due to the fact that I myself tend to be loud). This loudness is sometimes labeled as an act of striving to receive something from God rather than trusting Him and His goodness to give it when we ask.

It is true that there is a misconception that volume and authority is the same thing, that the louder you pray the more likely it is that things will happen. I want to suggest that this misconception is not always the motivation behind people praying loudly. Some people are just loud. Loudness is not a manifestation of God, per se. Some of that excitement can be restrained, and sometimes should be. However, what I'm addressing here is the offense, not any particular group or setting where discreetness, for whatever the reason, is encouraged. I do have to add that there are times when the Lord specifically uses loud noises to move things in the Spirit. There are many examples of this in Scripture, such as the walls of

Jericho falling at the sound of the loud shout by the people. Another example is in Acts 4:24 when the Apostles *"lifted up their voice,"* or raised their sound, in prayer. I have heard people release a shout at times and there is a real anointing of God at work through it.

Father Nash, an intercessor for Charles Finney, and a group with Father Nash were once in travail at an inn for a city. They had been praying and groaning for three days straight without eating anything, and the innkeeper feared for their health. Charles assured the innkeeper that they were in a deep place of prayer and in no danger to their health. Their prayers, as unbalanced as they seemed, were effectual in Charles Finney's ministry through which many would be "soundly converted."

Frank Bartleman's God-given desperation for revival led him to fast, and many, including his wife, feared he would fast himself to death. His intercession is believed by many to have impacted and even helped to birth the Azusa Street Revival. The fruit that is attributed to the intercession of these men is very great. They were barely known in their day, and many others who prayed along with them are still unknown. Unfortunately, these kinds of expressions have also been exaggerated by others or have been done from the flesh. What I am pointing out is that the moving of the Spirit is offensive to the mind that is set on the things of the earth.

Life In His Presence

In regards to the question of whether Day and Night prayer is balanced, I'd say that God's balance measurements are probably different than ours. Throughout history there have been decade-long prayer meetings that did not break through the night. Our society has many 24/7's that go unchallenged (grocery stores and businesses), so why is the thought of 24/7 prayer of concern to Christians? Under King David's leadership this became a norm in the Tabernacle of David. The Moravians are a respected group of radical Christians through whom many believe that the modern-day missionary movement was launched. They started a prayer meeting that lasted over a hundred years day and night. Their response to Jesus' teaching--that God avenges His elect who cry out to Him day and night--came with much fruit. The Methodist denomination came forth as fruit from the labors of the Moravians.

In the past decade or two, through the renewals and outpourings of the Spirit, there has been much teaching about the here-and-now realities of the Kingdom. I believe the Lord has been emphasizing these truths. However, some have understood that message and that emphasis from the Lord as meaning that He has done everything so that we don't have anything else to do. Some think that we already have everything and don't need to ask Him for more. But that is not true. Although it is true that we are not to do things on our own strength and that He has given us every spiritual blessing in the heavenly places, it is equally true that there is participation that the Lord is inviting us into and there is a way to appropriate those heavenly blessings that comes through ASKing, not from apathy. The truth that the Lord has been highlighting does not contradict His own invitation extended to us to ask, but it addresses the position of our hearts as sons and not as orphans to access those things that have been freely given to us.

There is labor involved on our part. It is by His finished work that we step confidently into the works that He has prepared for us (Ephesians 2:10). This work is easier than work we do in our own strength, but there is still labor involved (Romans 16:12; Colossians 1:29). Many of the apostles experienced this labor, calling themselves fellow laborers (1 Corinthians 16:16; Philemon 1:1). There is pleasure and even enjoyment in much of the labor, and much of that labor is intercession (Galatians 4:19). There is also, however, mourning in that labor. The Lord Jesus suffered on the cross and even now His heart aches for the lost and for the oppressed. This labor I'm writing of is one of partnering with His heart. God is full of emotions, and we will begin to feel those emotions when we participate in the invitation to be with Him where He is, to make intercession.. There is great joy in this and even a promise of glory throughout the scriptures (Philippians 3:10; Romans 8:17-18).

Life In His Presence

Effectual Prayer

There are times in intercession when the tangible power of God shows up in a person's prayer and God is empowering that prayer. It is the Spirit praying through a person. During experiences like these some people raise the volume of their voices, others continue to pray as they normally do as they become aware of the presence and power of God. Everyone responds differently, and no response is better than the other. *"The effective, fervent prayer of a righteous man avails much"* (James 5:16b).

This power in intercession will sometimes come as a burden from the Lord, something that one cannot shake but constantly thinks about. It may be a longing to see some kind of resolution or for justice to be executed. The Burden of the LORD would come upon prophets and they would prophesy. Not only would they prophesy but they would also pray. When the weight of what is on God's heart comes on us, there also comes a grace for us to agree with Him until we see the manifestation of our prayers. We can tap into the manifest presence for a moment as the anointing for effective prayer comes upon us. Also, we can actually carry a burden with the Lord until we see it through.

"And shall God not avenge His own elect who cry out day and night to Him though He bears long with them? I tell you that He

The Glory of Intercession   *Chapter 6*

will avenge them speedily. Nevertheless, when the Son of Man comes, will He really find faith on the earth?"

Luke 18:7-8

Jesus said that God will avenge His elect who cry out day and night, and that He will do so speedily. People could be laboring faithfully in intercession for years and finally, in a matter of days, weeks, and months see the unfolding of what they had been praying for. Many will get burdens for family members, for cities, groups of people, nations, and even continents. I have often asked God to give me His burden for diverse issues if I find that my heart is cold towards them. I want to be sensitive and in agreement with His heart. I don't want to pass by poverty, lost souls, injustices, and continue on my way as though everything were just fine. I want to feel what He feels and to be moved with what moves His heart.

There are times when a burden of prayer will come over an individual or a group and will remain until there has been a breakthrough in the spirit, even if the breakthrough has not manifested in the natural. He has given us an assurance that comes with prayer before we even see the answer: *"If we ask anything according to His will, He hears us. And if we know that He hears us, whatever we ask, we know that we have the petitions that we have asked of Him"* (1 John 5:14-15).

Life In His Presence

Every individual is called to a life of intimacy with God; every believer is called to a life of effectual prayer. To be loved by God and to love Him in return is our first and foremost assignment on the earth. How this plays out in our lives individually will look different, but everyone is called to the place of prayer. There are three specific disciplines that Jesus taught about with the implication that they would be practiced by His followers (Matthew 6). They were: Giving, Praying, and Fasting. He did not say, "If" you do these but *"When"* you do these. Intercessory prayer is not a ministry reserved for a select few; God has called the whole ecclesia (church) into this honor of ruling with Christ from heavenly places. He sat us with Him not just for us to enjoy the view, but also to interact and participate with Him in what we see. None of the times that diverse callings and gifting are mentioned in Romans 12, 1 Corinthians 12, and Ephesians 4, is "intercessor" or "praying grandma" mentioned. Why? This position of intercession is for every believer to participate in. It is for the apostle, prophet, evangelist, pastor, teacher, businessman, stay-at-home mom, fireman, doctor--everyone.

The Glory of Intercession

Though times of prayer may not seem glorious, there is more to the Glory than goose-bumps. It is possible to be in the manifest presence of God and not even feel or experience it at first. Jacob realized that he had been in the presence of God in Bethel and said, *"Surely the LORD is in this place, and I did not know it"* (Genesis 28:16). Though intercession may not always feel powerful, God avenges His own elect who cry out. The dominion of Christ is advanced on the earth through the prayers of the saints. Though they may not seem glorious, prayers mixed with incense and fire are actually hurled back down to the earth releasing the purposes of God (Revelation 8:3-5).

The greatest act of intercession on the earth was the Cross, and that act is the foundation to all other intercession. When Jesus prayed to the Father before He went to the Cross, He said, *"And now, O Father, glorify Me together with Yourself, with the glory which I had with You before the world was"* (John 17:5).

I believe that the glory that He had with the Father before the world was created is the same that we see in Revelation 13:8 and 5:1-10: *"...the Lamb slain from the foundation of the world." "...Behold, the Lion of the tribe of Judah, the Root of David, has prevailed to open the scroll and to loose its seven seals. And I looked and behold in the midst of the throne and of the four living creatures, and in the midst of the elders, stood a Lamb as though it had been slain, having seven horns and seven eyes, which are the seven Spirits of God sent out into all the earth..."* He is the Lamb slain before the

Life In His Presence

foundation of the world on the Cross and continues as the resurrected Christ.

Intercession is an act of laying one's life down. This does not seem glorious, but in the Kingdom there is no higher honor than that of being a servant. Father Nash is not the well-known revivalist--he laid down his life for another man's ministry and success. This is the Glory of Intercession, being seated together with Christ in the heavenly places, and from there serving our brothers and His bride, the church.

Chapter 7

Experiencing the Living Word

Fellowship with the Living Word

"*In the beginning was the Word and the Word was with God, and the Word was God, He was with God in the beginning... and the word became flesh and dwelt among us*" (John 1:2, 14). And the Word was crucified: "*Sacrifice and offering you did not desire, but a body you have prepared for me... Behold, I have come--in the fullness of the book it is written of Me--to do Your will*'" (Hebrews 10:5, 7). In three days He was raised from the dead. After He had by Himself purged our sins, He sat down at the right hand of the Majesty in the Heavens, waiting till His enemies are made His footstool (Hebrews 1). The Word raised us up together and made us sit together in heavenly places in Christ Jesus. There He is able to save to the uttermost those who come to God through Him, since He ever lives to make intercession for them. We can have

Life In His Presence

fellowship with the Father and His Son Jesus Christ by the Holy Spirit dwelling in us. The Word became flesh, dwelt among us, died, rose again, raised us with Him, and ever lives to make intercession for us. We cannot have fellowship with someone who is dead, but He is Alive and we can now experience the Living Word.

"That which was from the beginning, which we have heard, which we have seen with our eyes, which we have looked upon, and our hands have handled, concerning the Word of life--the life was manifested and we have seen and bear witness, and declare to you that eternal life which was with the Father and was manifested to us--that which we have seen and heard we declare to you, that you also may have fellowship with us; and truly our fellowship is with the Father and with His Son Jesus Christ. And these things we write to you that your joy may be full."

1 John 1:1-4

John had fellowship with the Father and with the Son. What about with the Holy Spirit? Much of what John says that he is doing is actually what the ministry of the Holy Spirit is. Jesus said that the Holy Spirit would take what belongs to the Father and what is His and declare it to us. He said that the Holy Spirit will not speak on His own authority but what He hears He will speak. John the Beloved was in a position of partnership with the Holy Spirit and was a mouthpiece for the Spirit of God. He engaged in fellowship with the Trinity through the Word that he heard and the Holy Spirit within Him declared. John's fellowship was with the Father, the Son, and the Holy Spirit. As a mouthpiece of the Holy Spirit, he writes, *"truly our fellowship"* (1 John 1:3).

We enter into fellowship through the spoken Word of God; this is how we hear, see, and handle with our hands the Word of life. The Holy Spirit hears and declares to us the realities of heaven manifesting them on the earth. When the Word is spoken, the reality of it comes forth into our realm and we can experience it. I am writing about more than just any time the Bible is read (though it can happen every time we read the Bible) but more specifically when the Holy Spirit is involved in the declared Word of God. God declared things in the beginning as the Spirit hovered over the surface of the deep, and the reality of heaven came forth into the earth and creation took place. The declared Word (rhema) releases faith (Romans 10:17) and brings the substance of things hoped for onto the earth (Hebrews 11:1).

Power in the Word

What I mean by the declared Word is that which the Holy Spirit is highlighting at the moment and He breathes on. It

Life In His Presence

will never contradict the written Word (logos) because the Holy Spirit will only speak what He hears and we can trust His hearing. If it contradicts the Bible, the logos, then it is not the Holy Spirit speaking. Most often He declares through the logos. His Word carries grace and power to be imparted into the hearer (Ephesians 4:29) and with that power will actually bring itself to pass. *"For as the rain comes down, and the snow from heaven, and do not return there, but water the earth, and make it bring forth and bud, that it may give seed to the sower and bread to the eater, so shall My word be that goes forth from My mouth; it shall not return to Me void, but it shall accomplish what I please, and it shall prosper in the thing for which I sent it"* (Isaiah 55:10-11).

Whenever Jesus told anyone to "go and sin no more," He was giving them the power to overcome sin and walk in righteousness. He was giving them the ability to turn from darkness to His marvelous light. Some of them did turn, such as the woman who had been a prostitute, who then worshipped Him with a grateful heart, washing His feet with her tears.

One time the Lord convicted me about the way that I had been leading people He had entrusted me to care for and teach. He spoke these words right to my heart: "Fathering is not controlling." Immediately I fell on the floor weeping. As I was on the floor, I knew that something in me had changed and from then on I was no longer the same. The Holy Spirit continues to teach me and help me to grow in the area of discipleship, but in that instant when His Word was declared to my heart, something came forth from heaven into my heart. His Ways began to manifest in me.

There was yet another time when the Lord spoke to me. He said, "Go, lay your hands on the sick and I will be glorified through mighty deeds and power." After the Lord said this to me I went to a city in Virginia with no specific plans to minister but only to receive from the Lord at a conference. To avoid the long drive home that night I asked someone I had just met if my friend and I could sleep on the floor of their house. They agreed to house us for the night. The next day in their community with their neighbors and later in their church the Lord opened a door for us to minister and preach. My friend and I witnessed many healings in that city after the Lord had spoken. Some of these healings included a blind eye opening, two people being healed of breathing conditions, and many others healed as the Lord revealed what they needed. The Lord continued to open doors after that to speak to diverse groups and churches where I have seen God heal many. Both of these encounters began with the whispers of the Holy Spirit to my heart, and they imparted the grace I needed to walk in what the Lord was calling me to.

God Speaks Today through His Word!

"God, who at various times and in various ways spoke in time

Life In His Presence

past to the fathers by the prophets has in these last days spoken to us by His Son, whom He has appointed heir of all things, through whom also He made the worlds; who being the brightness of His glory and the express image of His person, and upholding all things by the word of His power, when He had by Himself purged our sins, sat down at the right hand of the Majesty on high, having become so much better than the angels, as He has by inheritance obtained a more excellent name than they."

Hebrews 1:1-4

What a privilege we have today that God speaks to us through His Son, and that the Holy Spirit declares the Word to us. In these last days He has spoken to us by His Son. The anointing in us (the Holy Spirit) leads us into all truth. We no longer need a prophet to hear God, or a priest to interpret the scriptures for us, for the Spirit of God teaches us all things. He is not done speaking; the Holy Spirit continues to speak to us today. Therefore the author of Hebrews quotes Psalm 95 saying, *"Today, if you will hear His voice, do not harden your hearts..."* (Hebrews 3:7).

There is a danger in pursuing encounter with God and not actually reading the Bible. We must know the written Word. Jesus is as much in the written Word as He is in the declared Word. This is a sure foundation, and without it we will be easily shaken. If we seek encounter with God and are not reading and meditating on the Word of God, we are on dangerous ground. Spirituality apart from the Word of God, apart from the logos, is not centered on Christ. When the rains and the winds come, the house built upon the sands of scripture-less experience will surely crumble (Matthew 7:24-27). And shakings <u>will</u> come. We need to be rooted in the written Word; if we are not, then we are very susceptible to deception.

Meditation

Most times when the Holy Spirit declares things to me it is through the written Word. I take the Word and read it over and over again. I meditate upon it until the Holy Spirit breathes through it into me. Two years before I heard the whisper of the Holy Spirit that told me to go and lay hands on the sick, I had meditated on Isaiah 53, Mark 16, and 1 Corinthians 2. The Lord brought those scriptures to life to me as I heard them, saw them, and handled them through meditation. Then by the faith that the Lord had imparted into me, I laid hands on the sick and they were healed. I write this to encourage you that you do not need a sovereign moment before you take hold of what is already available in the Word. The sovereign event you need happened 2000 years ago on the Cross. We now have access to take the logos and meditate on it until the Holy Spirit takes what we are meditating on and opens it up to us, giving us faith to

Life In His Presence

appropriate the reality in those verses.

When we get filled with the logos it is like getting filled with gun powder. Sometimes it is exciting while other times it may feel very dry. But we are being filled with potential for an explosive encounter with God that will tear down strongholds in our way of thinking and fill us with the power of God. When the Holy Spirit breathes His fire on the logos in your heart, you get an unquenchable flame. We need the Word of God to be written in our hearts. David so treasured the written Word that he hid it in his heart. I have actually purposed in my heart to memorize entire books of the Bible and have so far memorized Hebrews, Ephesians, and some of James. I may not be able to quote the whole thing at the moment since it has been some time since I memorized it, but I can still quote large portions of these books. I write this to encourage you to commit the Word to memory and to hide it in your heart.

Jesus said that where a man's treasure lies there his heart will lie also. When we esteem and value the Word, our hearts will rest there in the Word. David describes the Word of God various times as honey on his lips. The way that bees make honey is by taking nectar and regurgitating it; the way that we turn the Word of God into honey in us is by taking it and regurgitating it, murmuring it in pleasure, repeating it over and over. The reason the Word was sweeter than honey to David is because he had so meditated upon it that it became his own

Experiencing the Living Word Chapter 7

rather than just letters on a scroll. You may not know this, but honey also is free of germs because it is not watered down. As we meditate upon the Word, impurities and defilements in our understanding are removed so that we, too, can be freed from "germs."

Meditation (in Hebrew, *śîyach* - to converse with oneself aloud; *hâgâh* - to murmur in pleasure or in anger) is the way that we partake of eternal realities. Honey is a substance that does not go bad. They recently found 2000-year-old honey in Egyptian pyramids that was still good and was not corrupted. This is how we download eternal heavenly realities into a temporal environment. When bees regurgitate nectar, they produce this substance called "honey"; when we regurgitate the scriptures, we get this wonderful thing called "faith": *"The substance of things hoped for, the evidence of things not seen"* (Hebrews 11:1); *"for faith comes by hearing and hearing by the word of God"* (Romans 10:17). When we read the scriptures, we get refreshed by them. It isn't until we meditate upon them, however, that they are written on our hearts and we truly partake of them as they become a part of us.

Writing the scriptures is another means into encounter. A friend of mine just finished writing through the whole New Testament and plans on writing the Old Testament. Anything that will keep us thinking on the Word and will place it at the forefront of our thoughts is worth partaking in. We can also

163

Life In His Presence

declare the Scriptures. When God kisses us with His Word, we can speak it in faith in agreement with Him to proclaim His Kingdom and Will (Matthew 6) manifesting on the earth.

We can even visualize the scriptures and use our imaginations to behold the Word rather than all the other things we can use our minds for. The imagination has been used greatly by the enemy, but it was created by God. I would encourage you to read verses that describe Jesus (like Revelation 1) and to actually picture Him in your mind. Also picture the Throne as described in Revelation 4, as well as Ezekiel chapters 1 and 10. The Lord may also take you up into encounter through this simple means of meditation.

"He who has My commandments and keeps them, it is he who loves Me. And he who loves Me will be loved by My Father, and I will love him and manifest Myself to him… If anyone loves me, he will keep My word; and My Father will love him, and We will come to him and make Our home with him."

John 14:21, 23

Jesus said these words to His disciples while He was still with them. There were aspects of Him that were yet to be manifested even though He walked with them in the flesh. On the Mount of Transfiguration Jesus manifested Himself to Peter, James, and John in a manner that not many had seen. Though

He was in the flesh, He would still manifest Himself in greater ways. Even so, now while He is not in the flesh, He continues to manifest Himself. When we treasure and keep His Word, not only is our heart there with that treasure, but He and His Father come and dwell in us.

Our Ability to Retain and Understand the Word

Jesus told His disciples that He had more to tell them that they would not be able to handle then, but that when the Spirit of Truth had come, He would lead them into all Truth (John 16). He had more of Himself to manifest to them, but they did not have, as Bill Johnson calls it, "the weight-bearing capacity" to carry and keep what He desired to share with them. They did not have the ability they needed to handle the manifestation of the Word, in order to receive what He had to give them. This is where the ministry of the Holy Spirit comes into play. Jesus told His disciples that it would be better for them that He should leave because then He would send the Holy Spirit and no longer would the Holy Spirit just be <u>with</u> them, but He would be <u>in</u> them.

We have received *"the Spirit who is from God, that we might know the things that have been freely given to us by God"* (1 Corinthians 2:12). As stated earlier, this is the ministry that John wrote He was participating in, the ministry of the Holy Spirit, declaring the manifested Word. Those things that have

Life In His Presence

been freely given to us are those things to which Jesus' Blood gave us access. Paul writes to the Ephesians, *"Blessed be the God and Father of our Lord Jesus Christ, who has blessed us with every spiritual blessing in the heavenly places in Christ"* (Ephesians 1:3). The Father has blessed us with every spiritual blessing in Christ, and the Holy Spirit reveals these blessings to us.

"But when He the Spirit of Truth has come, He will guide you into all truth; for He will not speak on His own authority, but whatever He hears He will speak; and He will tell you things to come. He will glorify Me, for He will take of what is Mine and He will declare it to you. All things that the Father has are Mine. Therefore I said that He will take of Mine and declare it to you."

John 16:13-15

God has so much for us that it is impossible for us to enter into it or be able to retain it without the Holy Spirit. Our understanding and our capacity are so limited that it takes God to know God. This is why Jesus said it would be better if He left, because He would send the Spirit to dwell in us Who would manifest Himself to them as He desired. When God speaks, He creates. Jesus wants His followers to experience and to be in touch with the realities of Heaven, so He sends His

Spirit to declare these realities in our hearts. He said, *"Father, I desire that they whom you have given to Me, that they would be with Me where I am that they may see my Glory"* (John 17:24).

"That He would grant you, according to the riches of His glory, to be strengthened with might through His Spirit in the inner man that Christ may dwell in your hearts through faith..." (Ephesians 3:16). The Holy Spirit strengthens us so that the Word, Christ, may dwell in our hearts through faith. We do not have "the weight-bearing capacity," but Holy Spirit does. The level of intimacy that God wants with us requires the work of Holy Spirit in us so that our fellowship may be with the Father and with the Son, Jesus Christ. The Word gives us faith and faith enables us to experience things unseen. Faith allows us to access heavenly blessings in Christ, *"In whom we have boldness and access with confidence through faith in Him"* (Ephesians 3:12). As we read the Word with faith, we can actually receive impartation of the realities being expressed in it. When we read with expectation, He encounters us. *"Let Him kiss me with the kisses of His mouth (Word), for your love is better than wine"* (Song of Songs 1:2). The Hebrew word used for "kiss" in this verse is the same word for equipping someone for battle. So we can say the verse this way, "Let Him equip me with the kisses of His Word." The Word of God actually empowers us; revelation of His love through His Word equips us to love Him and others.

Receiving from God's Word like a Child

When you read the Bible, read it as though someone were laying hands on you and praying for you. Read it expecting the peace and love you experience when someone gives you a hug or a kiss. Your experience in His Word will dramatically change as you approach the Word as being alive rather than just words on a page that you can use to change your life. We don't use the Word to change us, the Word does it Himself. He is not a tool to improve our lives; He is a person that will change us as we get around Him.

Encounter equips us. If the Word was dead, there would be no way to encounter Him except through vain imaginations. But the Word is alive so that we can experience the Living Word. We can see, handle with our hands, hear, and taste the Word of Life that will manifest Himself to us. We just need hearts of flesh that will reverberate with the vibrations of His Word. We need the hardness of our hearts to be removed so that our senses may be restored. When the Word manifests Himself, the dullness and insensitivity of our hearts can and will keep us from the appropriate response to the frequencies of His Word. God said through Isaiah that He is looking to dwell in one *"who is poor and of a contrite spirit, and who trembles at [His] Word"* (Isaiah 66:2b). When He speaks, we need to be aligned to His frequency and tremble. We carry His frequency, His Glory, with a broken heart and a contrite spirit.

Experiencing the Living Word   *Chapter 7*

"In the beginning was the Word, and the Word was with God, and the Word was God. He was in the beginning with God. All things were made through Him, and without Him nothing was made that was made...." (John 1:1-2). When God spoke the Word in the beginning, matter formed in the frequency of what He spoke. If He said birds, there were birds. Even so today, when our hearts vibrate with His Word, the heavenly reality being declared is formed in us.

It is important that we believe the Scriptures and not question their validity or their ability to impart the revelation of Jesus to us. The Israelites doubted the Word in the wilderness and did not enter into His rest but died in the wilderness. God wants to manifest Himself to us, but we will be living in disobedience and our hearts will be hardened if we give room to doubt and unbelief. Read Hebrews 3 & 4 and you will see how the Israelites in the wilderness missed out on what the Holy Spirit was declaring. *"For indeed the gospel was preached to us as well as to them; but the word which they heard did not profit them, not being mixed with faith in those who heard it"* (Hebrews 4:2). The Word needs to be mixed with faith in our hearts for it to profit us. For *"without faith it is impossible to please Him, for he who comes to God must believe that He is [who He says He is, what He says goes] and that He is a rewarder of those who diligently seek Him"* (Hebrews 11:6).

Life In His Presence

God is sovereign and has put the Scriptures together through human vessels. Some of you may be called to research and prove the validity of the Bible, and it is beneficial to have some understanding of how it came together. But let's not get caught up on whether it's the best version or most accurate or the fact that there are other books that didn't make it into the canon and miss the Living Word. Some of these genuine concerns are no longer genuine in Christ when they take our focus from Jesus so that we can no longer simply read and enjoy the Word. We need to let the Spirit convince us rather than trying really hard to figure things out.

Let us be childlike in our faith in the Scriptures--Jesus said it, the prophets said it, and the Apostles said it, so let's receive it. If not, let's believe Him for the sake of the works themselves (John 14:11), the works of the Holy Spirit that have drawn us to Him. Pride and faith in human wisdom as opposed to the wisdom of Christ will not work in the Kingdom. If you find those in your heart, repent and seek the Lord while He may be found. *"The entrance of [His] words gives light; it gives understanding to the simple"* (Psalm 119:130). This issue of doubt is a big stumbling block, and this pride sees Jesus and His Word as a rock of offense. I plead with you to get over yourself and believe.

Experiencing the Living Word   *Chapter 7*

Approaching the Word Made Flesh

Another challenge that we can face in searching the Scriptures is the dilemma the Pharisees found themselves in when the Word of Life was standing right in front of them. They read the scriptures to become knowledgeable but not to encounter God. This is a problem because *"knowledge puffs up, but love builds up"* (1 Corinthians 8:1). Jesus said to the Pharisees *"You search the Scriptures, for in them you think you have eternal life; and these are they which testify of Me. But you are not willing to come to Me that you may have life"* (John 5:39-40). They searched the Scriptures and missed the Living Word. Our motivation in searching the Scriptures will greatly affect our experience in them. Let's not get caught up in going deep into the Scriptures and growing in understanding at the expense of encountering Jesus. Let's go deep into the Scriptures and grow in wisdom and understanding, but let us not lose sight and miss the Kisses of His Word. Let's go deep into the Living Word remembering that He gives understanding to the simple that is so much better than any understanding we could come up with on our own.

Whenever you read the Bible and a certain verse seems to have life on it, the Lord is highlighting that verse for you-- these are the Kisses of His Word. At times like that, take a couple of minutes to meditate on that verse rather than continuing to read. Take some time to regurgitate it. Read it

Life In His Presence

over and over and ask the Lord to speak to you. When He kisses us with His Word, it then becomes our responsibility to enjoy Him, *"for His love is better than wine"* (Song of Songs 1:2). When He is drawing us, it is then our responsibility to run together (Song of Songs 1:4) with the Holy Spirit into the deep things.

Make the verse a personal prayer to the Lord. If I'm reading Psalm 42 and verse 8 comes alive to me, I could thank God that He commands His loving-kindness over me, and I could ask Him for more. If verse 7 jumps out at me, I can ask God to take me deeper. "Lord, deep calls unto deep, and I ask that You will take me deeper. I ask that you will let me hear Your Deep calling out to me, give me longing, grant me the gift of hunger, let me no longer be satisfied in the shallow but make me desperate so that I'll go deeper into You." In this I turned Psalm 42:7 into a prayer and made it a dialogue between God and me. I can be sure that He will respond to His Word.

The Scriptures in the Tabernacle of David were sung. We can sing the Word of God and enter into the melodies of heaven even if we cannot keep a tune. The presence of God is the context from which to go deep in the Word. There in the manifest presence of God, where the Ark of the Covenant was, priests sang the Scriptures as incense pleasing to the Lord. Even so today we can sing the Scriptures and worship God in the presence of the indwelling Spirit. We can enter into the song of the Spirit who searches the deep things of God and makes them known to us (1 Corinthians 2:9-10).

I often will pray in tongues for ten to fifteen minutes before reading the Bible. Paul said that when we pray in the Spirit we speak mysteries (1 Corinthians 14). I pray in the Spirit and believe the Lord for revelation of those mysteries as I read the Scriptures. *"It is the Glory of God to conceal a matter, but the glory of kings to search out a matter"* (Proverbs 25:2). God has concealed it <u>for</u> us not <u>from</u> us. He wants us to search it out, to jump in with the Holy Spirit as He searches the deep things of God. He wants us to partake of the mystery. Again, He has reserved it <u>for</u> us not <u>from</u> us. *"But we speak the wisdom of God in a mystery, the hidden wisdom which God ordained before the ages for our glory"* (1 Corinthians 2:7). This mystery is what was accomplished on the Cross and how that affects us, which is what all the Scriptures are pointing to.

Holy Entertainment

Sometimes we have to rearrange our schedules with our priorities in mind, or else those things that are really important will continue to be put aside so that we can do whatever is most pressing. Television and entertainment can be more pressing at times than reading the Bible or quieting our heart to hear God speak. This is a problem in our generation, especially since so much time is spent being entertained and on meditating on what we were entertained by. Whether it is a board game, video game, or TV show, we will find ourselves thinking about what we have seen throughout the day. What we are doing then is called meditation and often times it is solidifying the message of this world in our hearts. It is no surprise then that our heart becomes hardened to hear God's voice or to believe His Word when we do hear it. The wisdom of this age so fills our minds and hearts that it becomes a greater influence on our decision making than the influence of God's Word and Spirit.

When you hear a song, do you not find yourself singing it or find it playing over and over in your mind? Radio and TV commercials always have catchy tunes because advertisers want you to meditate on their agenda. This is also what the enemy is after. As a culture we have meditated so much on Hollywood that we know all the actors' names, their lifestyles, what they like to eat, and yet we don't know who Manoah is in the Bible. The Lord wired our brains for meditation and gave us an imagination to gaze on His Beauty.

This is why we need Holy entertainment. By this I don't mean good Christian movies or music, though those are good things. I'm talking about experiencing the pleasures of God so that we are caught up in meditation, murmuring in pleasure the Glory of God. I'm talking about the kind of entertainment that David enjoyed when he said, *"You will show me the path of life; in Your presence is fullness of joy; at Your right hand are pleasures forevermore"* (Psalm 16:11).

There will always be pressing things and desires in our lives, whether it is work, friends, escaping our problems through entertainment, etc. There will always be something to which we can give our attention and our affections. For this reason I encourage you to determine an hour of each day that you will set aside to experience God. If you have more time than that, then by all means use it to encounter God. Pray in the Spirit on your drive to work. Get up an hour early to read the Word. Spend some time worshiping the Lord and delighting in His presence. Whatever you do, set it in your heart to seek the Lord and for that time do not allow other pressures to get in the way. If there is a real emergency, you may have to deviate from your plan. However, many things will seem like emergencies when you try to be with the Lord, so determine to deal with those after you *seek first the Kingdom and His righteousness* (Matthew 6:33).

The Word of Life transforms us and defines us. For most of our lives we have been defined by the words of our parents, family, teachers, peers, entertainment, as well as our own words in agreement. But Jesus said that the Truth will set us free. It will define us and make us like Himself. Our tongue has the power of life and death, and we can agree with either one. So what are we waiting for? Let's encounter the Living Word. Let's leave this temporal reality and step into the eternal

Life In His Presence

pleasures that are in His Word. Let's allow the Truth of His Word to set us free and to identify who we are as we align our receptors to His Frequencies, as we are transformed from glory to Glory until we become a living epistle for our generation (2 Corinthians 3:3).

Chapter 8

The Way Everlasting

"Search me, O God, and know my heart; try me, and know my anxieties; and see if there is any wicked way in me, and lead me in the way everlasting."

Psalm 139:23-24

The Way of God is His Glory. It carries the full weight of His person, who He is. Many people desire and enjoy the benefits of His presence but they themselves do not partake of the fruit in it. For example, many enjoy the Lord's Kindness and Mercy, yet they themselves do not become kindness and mercy to those around them. They do not realize that everything in this world will perish except for those qualities that come from an Eternal Kingdom that cannot be shaken, so they spend their lives striving to attain some earthly reputation and an earthly treasure. Only those things that reflect His image will remain (1 Corinthians 13:8, 13). Pride, selfishness, greed,

Life In His Presence

anger, lust, etc., are temporary solutions to convenience ourselves. The fruits of the Spirit (Galatians 5:22) are selfless responses that have an eternal reward.

We are seeking and receiving an eternal kingdom, which cannot be shaken (Hebrews 12:28). Our life on earth has eternal consequence and our works here will be tested (1 Corinthians 3:12-15). Let those things that are of eternal value drive us forward, let us set our minds on things above where Christ is seated (Colossians 3:1). Do you want to live in a way that is eternal? *And this is eternal life, that they may know You, the only true God, and Jesus Christ whom You have sent* (John 17:3). Jesus is the Way!

Jesus is the Way

Hebrews 1:3 says that Jesus *"is the brightness of His [the Father's] Glory, the express image of His person."* He is the exact representation of the Father, and He has called us to be the same. We were made to display His likeness, to carry His image (Genesis 1:26; Colossians 3:10).

What was Jesus emanating? What was the light that proceeded from His being here on earth? It was the Way of the Father. It was the likeness of God that Jesus was emanating. He came and served as a humble servant. He came to earth shining Meekness, Humility, Kindness, Mercy, Compassion, Justice, Patience, Joy, Goodness, Self-control, Faithfulness, and Love.

The Way Everlasting Chapter 8

This is His Way.

This is what Jesus reflected, the light that the world rejected. *"In Him was life, and the life was the light of man. And the light shines in the darkness, and the darkness did not comprehend it"* (John 1:4-5). This light shines beyond actions and words but into the depths of the human heart. Those in darkness want nothing to do with that which exposes and makes their wickedness manifest (Ephesians 5:13). *"This is the condemnation, that the light has come into the world, and men loved darkness rather than light, because their deeds were evil"* (John 3:19).

Jesus was speaking to a teacher of the law, Nicodemus, when He declared the condemnation of those who loved the darkness rather than the light. The Law addressed outward deeds but was powerless to transform people on the inside (Hebrews 7:18-19). It was because their deeds were evil that they rejected the light. Many of the ones who rejected Him were those who apparently did everything right, the religious of His day, but His Word discerns not simply the outward actions we do but especially the intentions and motives of the heart (Hebrews 4:12-13).

Reflecting His Image

Many times when we hear the word "Glory" in the context of the manifest presence of God, we think of things like

Life In His Presence

Moses' face shining or a cloud filling the temple. But what was the light that was coming forth from Moses' face? It was the same light that Christ came shining, but in Moses' days the Israelites rejected it. *"For indeed the gospel was preached to us as well as to them; but the word which they heard did not profit them [the Hebrews in the wilderness,], not being mixed with faith in those who heard it"* (Hebrews 4:2). Why was it so disturbing to the people of Israel? It exposed the inner workings of their hearts. It is the same light that Isaiah saw when he said, *"Woe is me, for I am undone! Because I am a man of unclean lips, I dwell in the midst of a people of unclean lips; for my eyes have seen the King, the LORD of Hosts"* (Isaiah 6:5).

Moses could boldly and humbly write about himself: *"Now the man Moses was very meek, more than all people who were on the face of the earth"* (Numbers 12:3). The reason he could say that about himself is that he was reflecting the Light. He radiated the likeness of God. That was the Light that offended his generation so that he covered his face with a veil (Exodus 34:29-35), and that same veil lies over those who have not yet entered into the New Covenant, *"the new and living way, which He [Jesus] consecrated for us, through the veil, that is His flesh"* (Hebrews 10:20). The same veil remains on those who have not stepped by faith through the finished work on the Cross.

God has an opinion, His presence has a conviction, and those who are not in agreement with Him despise who He is. If you think that you love God, but hate your brother, you are not in agreement with Him and have deceived yourself (1 John 4:20). This is the essence of Light, the essence of who He is: *"God is Love"* (1 John 4:16).

How many people talk about love, and think they actually are in agreement with Him. The Scriptures paint a picture of Love that most people are completely unaware of as they romanticize the substance of love to be something that benefits them without costing them their lives. They want something kind and cuddly, something that is completely gentle towards them or even towards others and the poor. But what about becoming that substance? What about being that gentle comfort to others? What about taking hold of that substance instead of leaving it as an ethereal concept floating around in the air while no one actually embodies it. Here is a painting of the kind of Love the scriptures talk about:

"Therefore if there is any consolation in Christ, if any comfort of love, if any fellowship of the Spirit, if any affection and mercy, fulfill my joy by being likeminded, having the same love, being of one accord, of one mind. Let nothing be done through selfish ambition or conceit, but in lowliness of mind let each esteem others better than himself. Let each of you look out not

Life In His Presence

only for his own interests, but also for the interests of others. Let this mind be in you which was also in Christ Jesus, who, being in the form of God did not consider it robbery to be equal with God, but made Himself of no reputation, taking the form of a bondservant, and coming in the likeness of men. And being found in appearance as a man, He humbled Himself and became obedient to the point of death, even the death of the cross."

Philippians 2:1-8

In how much agreement are we really with this substance, this Love? It's much easier to be a recipient of such love and such selflessness from others, but what about being a reciprocator of such Love? It's easy to dream of a better world, but who will come into agreement with the Light that brings evil to shame, and turn to follow this Light in the Everlasting Way. *"Nevertheless, when one turns to the Lord, the veil is taken away..."* (2 Corinthians 3:16). No matter how much you try, you will find yourself lacking this Love and unable to reciprocate it without turning to the Lord. You will never be able to reflect a Light you are not beholding. You must be willing to take the "burn" of beholding true Beauty and allowing Him to transform you into His likeness from glory to Glory (2 Corinthians 3:16-18).

The Light Makes Manifest

The light *"makes manifest"* (Ephesians 5:13) exactly what is in the heart of an individual: greed, selfish ambition, pride, lust, etc. When those things are exposed, when Light comes in, we have a choice to make. Will we hide and be condemned, or will we agree with the essence of this Light and turn from our wicked ways and walk in the Light? *"For [if you are in Christ] you were once darkness, but now you are light in the Lord. Walk as children of light, for the fruit of the Spirit is in all goodness, righteousness, and truth..."* (Ephesians 5:8-9). Adam and Eve hid from this light, and most of humanity has followed in their footsteps.

Jesus further exposes man's ways in opposition to His own when He challenges the standards of righteousness in His day. Those perverse standards are still the same today for many who trust in their own righteousness and not Christ's.

"For I say to you, that unless your righteousness exceeds the righteousness of the scribes and Pharisees, you will by no means enter the kingdom of heaven. You have heard that it was said to those of old, 'You shall not murder, and whoever murders will be in danger of the judgment.' But I say to you that whoever is angry with his brother without a cause shall be in danger of the judgment. And whoever says to his brother, 'Raca!' shall be in danger of the council. But whoever says,

Life In His Presence

'You fool!' shall be in danger of hell fire... You have heard that it was said to those of old, 'You shall not commit adultery.' But I say to you that whoever looks at a woman to lust for her has already committed adultery with her in his heart... Furthermore it has been said, 'Whoever divorces his wife, let him give her a certificate of divorce.' But I say to you that whoever divorces his wife for any reason except sexual immorality causes her to commit adultery; and whoever marries a woman who is divorced commits adultery.' Again you have heard that it was said to those of old, 'You shall not swear falsely, but shall perform your oaths to the Lord.' But I say to you, do not swear at all: neither by heaven, for it is God's throne; nor by the earth, for it is His footstool; nor by Jerusalem, for it is the city of the great King. Nor shall you swear by your head, because you cannot make one hair white or black... You have heard that it was said, 'An eye for an eye and a tooth for a tooth.' But I tell you not to resist an evil person. But whoever slaps you on your right cheek, turn the other to him also... You have heard that it was said, 'You shall love your neighbor and hate your enemy.' But I say to you, love your enemies, and bless those who curse you, pray for those who spitefully use you and persecute you, that you may be sons of your Father in heaven; for He makes His sun rise on the evil and on the good, and sends rain on the just and on the unjust. For if you love those who love you, what reward have you? Do not even the tax collectors do the *same?... Therefore you shall be perfect just as your Father in heaven is perfect."*

(Matthew 5:20-22, 27-28, 31-36, 38-39, 43-46, 48)

His words speak for themselves!

After all but one of these six challenges, Jesus teaches an appropriate response. Concerning murder in the heart, He teaches that we first reconcile with our brother before we worship. If someone has something against you, for which you are guilty, you are to humble yourself, agree with them, and apologize (Matthew 5:23-26). Concerning adultery in the heart, Jesus teaches that we cut off anything that causes us to stumble. If your iPhone causes your eye to sin, crush it with a hammer and throw it away (v. 29-30). Concerning oaths, He teaches that we are not to swear at all but are to be faithful to keep our words (v. 37). Concerning an evil person, He teaches that we are to lay down our lives and not resist the plundering of our goods (v. 40-42) (Hebrews 10:34). Concerning our enemies, "those who hate us and spitefully use and persecute us" (v. 44), He teaches us to love them, to bless them, and to pray for them that we may be sons of our Father (v. 44-45) and that we may be those who walk in His ways.

Life In His Presence

The Hidden Life

We are to live before the audience of One. The truth is that things done before the Lord are usually not brought to the spotlight before men whose eyes are fixed on the temporary. Light is not always understood or appreciated (John 1:5). Many may see it, but few will want to entertain the light, for it is neither valued nor understood by them. When people see that you do not indulge in their sinful ways, it is many times offensive and even repulsive to them. What they see is blinding and even bothersome to those whose deeds are of the darkness.

Jesus teaches us to live a secret life before the Father, not necessarily hiding from men, but doing things primarily for the Father to see rather than to impress men. We are actually exhorted to let our light so shine before man that they glorify our Father in heaven. When we exude Christ-likeness, to some it will be a fragrance of life and to others it will be a fragrance repulsive to them (2 Corinthians 2:14). When we let our light shine we are allowing something that we value shine forth in an environment where those values may not be shared.

This light we are to reflect, is not earthly and it is not outward, but it is an internal reality. It is not buying an expensive tuxedo that says Jesus on it or even wearing a smile on our faces. It is the true overflowing of Love from our hearts. It is gained and displayed in a place that is hidden to the natural eye. It is hidden in the secret place and it is to the Father's delight. It is primarily for His pleasure rather than for our own elevation. Some people may never see the good intentions of your heart, but the Father will. Others with impure motives may be promoted at times while you may remain in the background. Your life becomes not about what you or others think about yourself but about what the Father thinks of you!

You begin to experience the hidden life that Jesus lived, *"Who, being in the form of God, did not consider it robbery to be equal with God, but made Himself of no reputation, taking the form of a bondservant, and coming in the likeness of men. And being found in appearance as a man, He humbled Himself and became obedient to the point of death, even the death of the cross"* (Philippians 2:6-8). Did you come to Christ to gain riches and have a good reputation? To be known as being a good person? Are you religious so that men can look up to you?

We can get so caught up in doing the right things and in fulfilling the appearance we feel we ought to have, that we don't ever actually exude Christ-likeness. We may fit the part to those eyes that see only outwardly but Christ is not truly formed in us. We may not yell vainly at the person who inconvenienced us, but our hearts may exude hatred and bitterness. Instead of saying it audibly with our mouths, we may smile outwardly while violently cursing them inwardly.

It is not enough to do good things, or to appear to be a good person or even a good Christian; we must know the Man

Life In His Presence

Jesus, the One who is the exact representation of the Father. We must behold Him and become like Him.

"For My thoughts are not your thoughts, nor are your ways My ways."

Isaiah 55:8

God's value system is different than ours. The mindset that is according to the flesh esteems temporal things while the mind that is set according to the Spirit esteems the things that are eternal. The mind that has not been renewed by the Spirit values things like money, good reputations, positions, gain (even if not justly), praise from men, instant gratification, etc. Some of these things are not bad, but the pride and selfishness in the human heart that longs for these are harmful to us and contrary to God's nature.

I recently heard a friend preach a sermon about the way a man changes when he falls in love, such as living in certain ways to please the woman he loves or doing things to catch her eye. In that same way, we also are to live to please the Lord, and what catches His eyes are those disciplines and acts which are done in secret (Read Matthew 6). What catches His eye are the inner workings of our hearts when we choose to love rather than to hate, when we choose to overlook offense rather than hold it against the individual.

The Beatitudes

In the Sermon on the Mount (Matthew 5-7) Jesus lays out for us the values of the Kingdom and spells out His Glory. Before Jesus taught on the mountain He had called Peter, Andrew, James, and John and said to them, *"Follow Me"* (Matthew 4:19,22). Jesus did what He saw His Father doing and invited His disciples to do the same with Him--to walk where He walked and to do what He did. In order for His disciples to walk well with Him, Jesus taught them the Way. What He really does in His teaching is to describe the way that He leads His own life, the guiding principles to every step He takes so that they too could take those steps.

Surrounding the Sermon are the works of power that Jesus performed. At the center of these acts of power was the essence from which overflowed such works. They overflowed from His Love and were evidence of the authority that He walked in as the Son of God. This teaching was imperative lest the disciples should walk in the power of God but not in His ways. Jesus warned that there would be those who would do so to their own destruction. Jesus said, *"Many will say to Me in that day, 'Lord, Lord, have we not prophesied in Your name, cast out demons in Your name, and done many wonders in Your name?' And then I will declare to them, 'I never knew you; depart from Me, you who practice lawlessness!'"* (Matthew 7:22-23). Not only did He declare that He never knew them but

Life In His Presence

also that they were those who practiced lawlessness. The Lord knows everything about everyone but is only intimately acquainted with those who spend time in His presence and who walk with Him, in His Way.

"And seeing the multitudes, He went up on a mountain, and when He was seated His disciples came to Him. Then He opened His mouth and taught them saying: 'Blessed are the poor in spirit, for theirs is the kingdom of heaven. Blessed are those who mourn, for they shall be comforted [parakaleo--to call near]. Blessed are the meek, for they shall inherit the earth. Blessed are those who hunger and thirst for righteousness, for they shall be filled. Blessed are the merciful, for they shall obtain mercy. Blessed are the pure in heart, for they shall see God. Blessed are the peacemakers, for they shall be called sons of God. Blessed are those who are persecuted for righteousness' sake, for theirs is the kingdom of heaven. Blessed are you when they revile and persecute you, and say all kinds of evil against you falsely for My sake.

Matthew 5:1-11

These are the Kingdom values: The poor are rich, the broken are desired, the meek are royal heirs, the hungry and thirsty are satisfied, the merciful are shown mercy, the pure are enlightened, the peace makers are adopted by God, and the persecuted are enthroned. Those who build their own kingdoms on earth receive nothing of value from it in eternity. Those who seek their own glory on earth find dissatisfaction on earth and destruction in eternity. Those who use the power of God for their own gain will hear Him say, *"I never knew you"* (Matthew 7:23). The Ways of God and His Glory are inseparable. We cannot pick one or the other.

Poor in spirit - When we acknowledge our desperate need for Him, then the riches of His Kingdom are readily available to us. **Mourn** - When we weep for the things that He also weeps for, He calls us near to Himself. **Meek** - When we use our strength to love, to serve, and to prefer others, He gives us the things that many use their strength to fight for. **Hunger and Thirst for Righteousness** - When we desire to be like Him, He nourishes us with the bread of revelation and gives us wine and milk from His table (Isaiah 55:1). **Pure in Heart** - When we devote all our heart, affections, and attention to Him, He opens our eyes to see Him. **Peacemakers** - When we live in a place of peace and it overflows to people and circumstances around us, He identifies us with Himself as His sons. **Persecuted for Righteousness' Sake** - When we are treated like the scum of the earth because of righteousness, He promotes us in His Kingdom into a place of authority.

Jesus experienced and embodied all of these. From His complete devotion to the Father He saw what the Father was doing and did it, which brought the Father Glory. And we are

Life In His Presence

likewise called to share in His nature to do what we see Him and the Father doing. He is Light and has made us to be like Him. He said, *"You are the light of the world. A city on a hill cannot be hidden. Nor do they light a lamp and put it under a basket, but on a lamp stand, and it gives light to all who are in the house. Let your light so shine before men, that they may see your good works and glorify your father in Heaven"* (Matthew 5:14-16).

Jesus identifies us with Himself when He calls us the light of the World. This is what we are to be--light. We are not to seek to bring attention to ourselves, but to reflect Him in such a way that when people see us they first think of Jesus and not of us. We should not hide for fear of what those in darkness will think of us if they find that we are not in agreement with them. Nor do we need to try really hard to shine; we already are light, and we don't strive to be bright or to show others that we are bright. Our job is simply not to hide it in a basket or anywhere else where it cannot be seen.

This is not something that we can initiate from our own ability and ingenuity. He has to make His face to shine on us. Since He has given us access to Himself, we can position ourselves to behold Him and become like Him. Rather than being empty flashlights trying to find some power in ourselves to shine forth His light, we can be mirrors that continually reflect His beauty because our gaze is set on Him (Psalm 27:4).

Give! Pray! Fast! In Secret - Openly Rewarded

In the Sermon on the Mount Jesus gives us disciplines that will actually position us to encounter Him. The disciplines spoken of in Matthew 6 are giving, praying, and fasting; He further teaches that the key is to do these in secret. These three disciplines are presented by Jesus as being normal Christianity. He did not say, "If you give.." He said, *"When you... give... pray... fast"* (Matthew 6). He did not present them as something we had to do, but as something we would do. He did not command us in Matthew 6 to give, pray, and fast; He simply communicated that this would be a natural result of following Him. He directed us on how we should express those disciplines so that they are most appealing to the Father. These can be done for our own conscience's sake, out of our desire for others to see, or out of our Love for God and desire to draw near to Him. If the motivation behind these disciplines does not come out of a place of Love for God primarily and Love for others secondarily, they are empty motions.

"Take heed that you do not do your charitable deeds before men, to be seen by them. Otherwise you have no reward from your Father in heaven... do not sound a trumpet before you as the hypocrites do in the synagogues and in the streets, that they may have glory from men. Assuredly, I say to you, they have their reward. But when you do a charitable deed, do not let

your left hand know what your right hand is doing, that your charitable deed may be in secret; and your Father who sees in secret will Himself reward you openly."

Matthew 6:1-4

There are actual rewards to giving, praying, and fasting. The reward is the knowledge of Christ. It is revelation of Jesus and Christlikeness. We encounter God through giving and come to know Jesus' faithfulness. The sacrifice in giving, when done before the Father, is multiplied and the reward we gain is greater then the cost we pay. We can only give what we have been given, so we must acknowledge that it wasn't ours to begin with, in order to be able to lay it down at His feet. Then we'll find that the Lord will still meet our own needs even with the loss. Because we acknowledge that it wasn't ours to begin with, we realize it was never meant to be used for our own gain. We can use what we've been given by God to partner with Him OR to build our own kingdom.

If we give out of our own abundance, all we can give is what man has to offer. By this I don't mean so much the amount that we can give or do give, but more the attitude of our heart in giving. If we give in pride, believing the gift we have provided out of our own resource will accomplish something great, we have limited that gift to man's ability as opposed to God's ability. What God has to offer is so much better than what man has to offer. The rich give out of their own resources. The poor in spirit, the ones who recognize that apart from Christ they have nothing of value to offer, give out of the storehouses of heaven what they could not afford. In simpler terms, a gift given in Love and Humility both greatly impacts the human heart and supplies the practical need of an individual. We are called to give what God has to offer. Jesus gave from the resources of heaven. He fed thousands on various occasions with just one individual's lunch, and they still had food left over after all had eaten and were satisfied!

God is not interested in what we can give Him. He deserves more than what we can give to Him. So He gives us from His supply that we may give back to Him.

"When you pray, go into your room, and when you have shut your door, pray to your Father who is in the secret place; and your Father who sees in secret will reward you openly."

Matthew 6:6

The next discipline that Jesus spoke of in Matthew 6 was prayer. He tells His disciples what <u>not</u> to do, in whose ways <u>not</u> to walk, and then He proceeds to tell them <u>what</u> to do. The Pharisees walked in the ways of man and therefore sought to please or impress men. Jesus walked in the ways of God and He sought to please the Father. He invited His disciples to do the same. He invited us into conversation with the Father.

Life In His Presence

"Our Father in heaven, hallowed be Your name. your kingdom come. Your will be done on earth as it is in heaven. Give us this day our daily bread. And forgive us our debts, as we forgive our debtors. And do not lead us into temptation, but deliver us from the evil one. For Yours is the kingdom and the power and the glory forever. Amen."

Matthew 6:9-13

It is hard to speak to someone who is either not listening or not responding. God didn't ask us simply to talk to Him, but also to listen to Him. He is listening, and He will respond. If we speak to God without any expectation that He will respond, prayer can be a boring thing. Without that expectation, most times prayer will be dry. It was never meant to be a monologue or only a journal entry. God wants to speak. He wants to interact with us. Hebrews 11:6 says, *"But without faith it is impossible to please Him, for he who comes to God [he who prays] must believe that He is, and that He is a rewarder of those who diligently seek Him."* He who comes to God must believe that He will respond and will therefore diligently seek Him. When prayer becomes an experience, then it will be enjoyable. Mel Tari shares in his book, *Like a Mighty Rushing Wind*, that in science we must experience to believe, but in the Kingdom we must first believe to experience.

How can we be like someone we don't know? And how

can we know someone we do not converse with? Jesus said *"My sheep hear My voice, and I know them, and they follow Me"* (John 10:27). It is through conversation that we get to know Him and by following Him that we get to know His ways. When we believe God, we experience Him. When we experience, we get to know Him.

"When you fast, anoint your head and wash your face, so that you do not appear to men to be fasting, but to your Father who is in the secret place; and your Father who sees in secret will reward you openly."

Matthew 6:17-18

Fasting is commonly used by many but primarily to be seen by peers as spiritual. Though this is a big temptation, it is not the purpose of fasting and it actually hinders the benefits and rewards that are promised with fasting. Seeing and understanding that temptation in His days, Jesus taught His disciples to look for the Father's approval and not men's.

Fasting is a major tool for sensitizing our spirits to the Father's will, to hear His voice with greater clarity. With all the clatter and all the distractions in this generation, turning off many of those things that call for our attention allows us to quiet down and receive from the Lord. As we restrain from momentary pleasures, even legitimate things such as food, we

Life In His Presence

make room for that which is eternal. We don't fast to earn something, for Jesus already paid the price, but we fast to position our hearts to hear what the Holy Spirit has to say. There is spiritual gain that is experienced through fasting, and it comes as the Holy Spirit reveals the things that have been freely given to us (1 Corinthians 2:12).

God has great plans for our lives. He wants to empower us and use us for His Glory and here is the Way: Intimacy. That is what we were really made for. Doing the works, and seeing God move in our lives, is meant to be a continuation of that intimacy. It is to flow out of intimacy and into intimacy. The works are supposed to proceed from us being near to God and are to be an expression that we do together with Him. We can walk in power and do great things without knowing Him, but then we will be missing the very purpose of our existence. God walked with Adam and Eve in the Garden and His desire to continue to do so with humanity has not changed. He has a Way, and has consecrated it for us (Hebrews 10:19) in order that we will actually walk with Him in it.

Fruit that Remains

"But a certain man named Ananias, with Sapphira his wife, sold a possession. And he kept back part of the proceeds, his wife also being aware of it, and brought a certain part and laid it at the apostles' feet. But Peter said, 'Ananias, why has Satan

filled your heart to lie to the Holy Spirit and keep back part of the price of the land for yourself? While it remained, was it not your own? And after it was sold, was it not in your own control? Why have you conceived this thing in your heart? You have not lied to men but to God.' Then Ananias, hearing these words, fell down and breathed his last. So great fear came upon all those who heard these things."

Acts 5:1-5

Ananias and his wife Sapphira tried to use the discipline of giving mentioned in Matthew 6 for their own glory. The results were not what they expected. Satan had filled their hearts to lie to the Holy Spirit because there was already a desire in their hearts to have a good reputation among men. How many times have we done "good" things to be approved of by men rather than by God? This carnal mindset led them to seek reward in this age, rather than in the age to come. Their treasure was of earth and so their hearts were set on the things that are earthly (Matthew 6:19-21); so they lived as mere men (1 Corinthians 3:3) and not from a heavenly standpoint.

In the manifest presence of God Ananias and his wife experienced an immediate judgment that many have not experienced but will experience in the Day of Judgment. They serve as a sign, just as Lot's wife, of what our response ought to be whether God is moving with power or not. When He has

Life In His Presence

been moving in a manifest way, the consequences are more immediate. Many today do acts as wicked as what Ananias and Sapphira did and even more wicked but do not receive such an immediate judgment, but they too will be judged if they don't repent. Moses' sister Miriam is also a sign to us. All of these were partaking of evil fruits in the midst of a move of God's Spirit: Lot's wife loved the world; Miriam was operating in selfish ambition; Ananias and Sapphira sought the praises of men and walked in deception. Their experience demonstrated how God feels towards such motivations and actions and how they are contrary to His Way.

The proof of what we are made of is the product of our life, what our life produces. Jesus warned His disciples about false prophets and said *"You will know them by their fruits"* (Matthew 7:16). More than somebody getting healed of cancer, God is glorified when the vessel used for healing is full of Love and that Love is imparted to the person being healed. That is *"bearing much fruit"* (John 15:8); when Christlikeness spreads, blossoms, and abounds, then God is glorified.

We don't do nice things to be kind; we do nice things because we are kind. We should agree with who Christ says we are and be kind, but we should not try to appear as something that we have no desire to be like in our hearts. We should not be hypocrites. If we do acts just to seem "good" to others, we are deceiving others and ourselves. But the Lord is not deceived, and we will reap what we have sown (Galatians 6:7). If we sow emptiness, we reap nothing. If we sow spite, we reap hatred. If anger, rage. If lies, deceit. If Love, we will reap Life. But you cannot sow what you do not have, and there is only One Way to get it.

There is a difference between fruits of the Spirit and disciplines that embody those fruits. Outward actions can be done without really having the fruit within. Empty actions will not reproduce fruit that is nonexistent. Only the fruit of the Spirit will have eternal significance in our lives; all others will pass away. That is why the Apostle Paul writes, *"Though I speak with the tongues of men and of angels... though I have the gift of prophecy, and understand all mysteries and all knowledge, and though I have all faith, so that I could remove mountains, but have not love, I am nothing. And though I bestow all my goods to feed the poor, and though I give my body to be burned, but have not love, it profits me nothing"* (1 Corinthians 13:1-4). Works, disciplines, and outward actions that are not done His Way do not bear fruit in our hearts or the hearts of others, and they do not profit us in eternity.

What is the eternal reward of which we are going to partake? The Bible teaches that prophecy, healings, etc., will cease. So what will remain? *"Love never fails. But whether there are prophecies, they will fail; whether there are tongues, they will cease; whether there is knowledge, it will vanish*

Life In His Presence

away... And now abide faith, hope, and love, these three remain; but the greatest of these is love" (1 Corinthians 13:8, 13). What we sow in the Spirit now on earth we will continue to reap for all eternity. Our faith, our hope, and our love in the present reality are eternal seeds. The fruit that we partake of on earth is the fruit that we will continue to partake of for all eternity. We are not meek on earth so that we can be arrogant in heaven. Nor are we gracious on earth so we can be greedy in heaven. Nor are we humble on earth so that we can build our own kingdom in heaven. There are great riches in heaven and the reward is great. We will shine the light of His Ways for all eternity. We will dwell continually in His Glory. We will walk in the Way Everlasting.

Jesus has made a way for us to be with Him! His desire is that we should dwell with Him and His Father, and that they should dwell with us (Psalm 27:4, John 17:24). *Jesus answered and said... "If anyone loves Me, he will keep My word; and My Father will love him, and We will come to him and make Our home with him* (John 14:23). As we acknowledge God's Goodness--His nature--by thanking and praising Him, we become active participants in the glorification and earthly manifestations of the Creator of the heavens and the earth. We get to enjoy Him and reflect His likeness! This is the glorious

The Way Everlasting   *Chapter 8*

ministry that we have been chosen for, to behold Him, to become like Him. The rest is just the overflow. We get to share in His sufferings but we also get to share in His joy. He has unveiled His everlasting Way (Hebrews 10:19-22). This is Life in His Presence!

Reference	Chapter #	Reference	Chapter #
Genesis 1:26	4, 8	1 Samuel 21	5
Genesis 28:16	6	2 Samuel 6:11-12	4
Genesis 32:24-30	2	1 Chron. 15:2, 27	4
Exodus 3	3	1 Chron. 16:28	2
Exodus 3:11, 14	1	1 Chron. 17:8	2
Exodus 4:1, 3, 10	1	1 Chron. 21:13	5
Exodus 4:13-14	1	Psalm 2	6
Exodus 5:21-23	1	Psalm 16	4, 5
Exodus 6:2-3, 6-12	1	Psalm 16:11	7
Exodus 14:11-12	1	Psalm 16:5	5
Exodus 16:18	4	Psalm 22	2
Exodus 16:3, 7, 9	1	Psalm 23	5
Exodus 16:20-30	1	Psalm 23:6	4
Exodus 25:12-14	4	Psalm 26:8	1, 2, 4
Exodus 32:1-10	1	Psalm 27:4	1, 4, 5, 8
Exodus 33	3, 4	Psalm 27:4, 8	5
Exodus 33:13, 18-19	1	Psalm 29:1-2, 11	2
Exodus 34:29-35	8	Psalm 34:1	2
Exodus 34:5-8	1	Psalm 34:8	5
Numbers 9	2	Psalm 36	4
Numbers 9:15-18	4	Psalm 37:4	5
Numbers 9:22-23	4	Psalm 42	5
Numbers 11	4	Psalm 42:4	2
Numbers 12:3	8	Psalm 42:7	7
Numbers 14:11	1	Psalm 46	1, 2, 4
Numbers 16	4	Psalm 47:1	2
Deut. 6-8	3	Psalm 68:34	2
Deut. 6:4-5	2	Psalm 84:1-2	4, 5
Deut. 8:12-14	3	Psalm 84:10	4
Deut. 8:3-6	1	Psalm 84:4	2, 4
Joshua 3:13, 17	4	Psalm 95	1
Joshua 6:1-5	4	Psalm 96:7	2
1 Samuel 1:24	4	Psalm 100:4	2
1 Samuel 4:4	4	Psalm 110	4, 6
1 Samuel 5:2-12	4	Psalm 119:130	7
1 Samuel 6:19-20	4	Psalm 133	3
1 Samuel 15:22-25	5	Psalm 139:1, 3	1
1 Samuel 16	3	Psalm 139:23-24	1, 8

Reference	Chapter #	Reference	Chapter #
Psalm 145: 15-16	5	Matthew 6	5, 6, 7, 8
Psalm 149:6	2	Matthew 6:1-21	8
Proverbs 1:7	1	Matthew 6:14	6
Proverbs 13:12	5	Matthew 6:21	5
Proverbs 18:21	6	Matthew 6:33	1, 7
Proverbs 25:2	7	Matthew 7	5
SOS 1:2, 4	2, 7	Matthew 7	7
SOS 5:10b	6	Matthew 7:16-23	8
Isaiah 6	2	Matthew 9	5
Isaiah 9:7	4	Matthew 10:8	3
Isaiah 11	3	Matthew 11:12	5
Isaiah 53	7	Matthew 18:15-20	6
Isaiah 55:6-8	1	Matthew 23:11	6
Isaiah 55:1-2	5	Matthew 25	3
Isaiah 55:10-11	7	Matthew 26:6-8	2
Isaiah 55:8	1, 6, 8	Mark 4:18-19	5
Isaiah 55:1	5, 8	Mark 16	7
Isaiah 57	6	Luke 7:37-38, 47	2
Isaiah 57:19	2	Luke 11:13	5
Isaiah 61	3	Luke 11:20	3
Isaiah 64	1	Luke 18:7-8, 10-14	6
Isaiah 64:4, 7	5	John 1:1-2	7
Isaiah 66:1-2	2	John 1:14	3, 7
Isaiah 66	5	John 1:4-5	8
Isaiah 66:2b	2, 7	John 10:10	6
Jeremiah 29:13	2	John 2:4	5
Jeremiah 31:32	1	John 3	6
Ezekiel 1 & 10	7	John 3:19	8
Hosea 4:6	5	John 3:8, 27	3
Nahum 1:3	1	John 4:10	5
Malachi 1:11	2, 4	John 4:10	5
Matthew 4:19, 22	8	John 4:24	2
Matthew 4:4	4	John 5:19	3
Matthew 5-7	8	John 5:39-40	7
Matthew 5: 6	1, 5	John 6:53-66	6
Matthew 5:18	4	John 7:16-18	3
Matthew 5:20-48	8	John 10:27	8
Matthew 5:44-45	6	John 14:11	7

Reference	Chapter #	Reference	Chapter #
John 14:21	7	1 Cor. 8:1	7
John 14:23	7, 8	1 Cor. 12	6
John 14:6, 8-9b, 15	1	1 Cor. 12:29-31	3
John 15:20	5	1 Cor. 12:31	3, 5
John 15:5	3	1 Cor. 13:1-13	8
John 15:8	8	1 Cor. 14	7
John 16:12	3	1 Cor. 16:16	6
John 16:13-15	7	2 Cor. 2:14	3, 8
John 16:14	1	2 Cor. 3:16	2, 8
John 16:14-15	4	2 Cor. 3:16-18	8
John 17:24	6, 7, 8	2 Cor. 3:17	3, 8
John 17:3	5, 8	2 Cor. 3:3	7
John 17:5	6	2 Cor. 3:7-11	4
Acts 2	3	2 Cor. 4:10, 17	5
Acts 3:19, 25b-26	5	2 Cor. 4:6-7	3
Acts 4	6	Galatians 2:20	3, 5
Acts 5:1-5	8	Galatians 4:19	6
Acts 5:12-16	3	Galatians 5	5
Acts 6:1-7	3	Galatians 5:22	8
Acts 8	3	Galatians 6:7	8
Acts 10	3	Ephesians 1:17-19	5
Romans 8	5	Ephesians 1:19-23	6
Romans 8:17-18	6	Ephesians 1:3	5, 7
Romans 10:17	2, 5, 7	Ephesians 2:19-22	3
Romans 11:22, 23	1	Ephesians 2:6, 10	6
Romans 12	6	Ephesians 3:12	7
Romans 16:12	6	Ephesians 3:16	3, 7
1 Cor. 1:24	1	Ephesians 3:16-19	3
1 Cor. 2	7	Ephesians 3:20	5
1 Cor. 2:12	7, 8	Ephesians 4	3, 6
1 Cor. 2:7	7	Ephesians 4:11-14	3
1 Cor. 2:9	1, 5	Ephesians 4:29	7
1 Cor. 2:9-10	1, 7	Ephesians 5:18	3
1 Cor. 3	3	Ephesians 5:8-9, 13	8
1 Cor. 3:16-17	5	Philippians 2:1-8	8
1 Cor. 3:3, 12-15	8	Philippians 2:8-11	6
1 Cor. 6	3	Philippians 3:10	5, 6
1 Cor. 6:17-20	5	Philippians 3:8, 21	5

Reference	Chapter #	Reference	Chapter #
Colossians 1:27	3, 4	Hebrews 10:20	2, 8
Colossians 1:29	6	Hebrews 10:34	8
Colossians 3:1-4	6	Hebrews 10:37	1
Colossians 3:1, 10	8	Hebrews 10:5	6, 7
Philemon 1:1	6	Hebrews 10:7	7
Hebrews 1:1-4	7	Hebrews 11:1	2, 7
Hebrews 1:3	1, 8	Hebrews 11:10	3
Hebrews 1:4, 13	6	Hebrews 11:16, 26	5
Hebrews 2:12	2	Hebrews 11:6	2, 5, 7, 8
Hebrews 3 & 4	7	Hebrews 11:8-10	5
Hebrews 3:7	7	Hebrews 12	1
Hebrews 3:7-9	1	Hebrews 12:1, 14	3
Hebrews 3:18-19	1	Hebrews 12:2	3, 5
Hebrews 4:10	1	Hebrews 12:28	8
Hebrews 4:11	2	Hebrews 13:15	2
Hebrews 4:16	6	Hebrews 13:8	1
Hebrews 4:2	3, 7, 8	James 1:17	1
Hebrews 4:4	8	James 1:6-7	5
Hebrews 5:4	6	James 3:14-18	3
Hebrews 6	5	James 4:3, 6	5
Hebrews 6:19	4	James 5:16b	6
Hebrews 7:12	4	1 Peter 1:11	5
Hebrews 7:23-25	4	1 Peter 2:6	5
Hebrews 7:18-19	4, 8	1 Peter 2:9	4, 6
Hebrews 7:22	1	2 Peter 1:3	5
Hebrews 8:1	6	1 John 1:1-4	7
Hebrews 8:13	4	1 John 1:5	2
Hebrews 8:9	1	1 John 2:15-16	5, 6
Hebrews 9:11	3	1 John 4:16, 20	8
Hebrews 9:4	4	1 John 4:19	1
Hebrews 10:1, 20	3	1 John 5:14-15	6
Hebrews 10:31	3	Revelation 1	7
Hebrews 10:10	6	Revelation 4	7
Hebrews 10:12	6	Revelation 5:1-10	6
Hebrews 10:13	6	Revelation 8:3-5	6
Hebrews 10:19	4, 8	Revelation 13:8	6
Hebrews 10:19-22	1, 8		

About the author:

From a young age Sebastian has been longing for more of God. What commenced as a journey to walk in the power of God turned into a continual desiring for His presence as happens when one encounters God, who is Love (1 Corinthians 12:31). In his search, Sebastian has seen the power of God work miraculously in his life and in the lives of others. Sebastian walks in an anointing to heal the sick and in the contagious joy that is in God's presence. He is a gifted preacher of the Word of God. Currently, Sebastian serves as a teacher and leader in the Missions and Prayer School (MAPS) in Fredericksburg, Virginia where he has been serving full-time at the Fredericksburg Prayer Furnace for several years. Sebastian Angulo is a licensed minister who has been traveling and ministering locally and internationally.

Sebastian is also a gifted violinist that ministers prophetically through music. He was raised in Puerto Rico and moved to the United States at the age of nine.

For more information visit:
www.facebook.com/sebastianangulominelly

THE PRAYER FURNACE
HOUSE OF PRAYER MISSIONS BASE

The Fredericksburg Prayer Furnace is a missional community of believers serving the greater Fredericksburg region and beyond in a tri-fold ministry as (a) a house of prayer, (b) a training center, and (c) a local and global missions sending base.

We have a congregation called Awakening Community Church, which serves as a local church, and is fully integrated with the FPF missions base. Our vision is for FPF to be a regional and international ministry in that it serves Christians in many churches (not just our own church) across our city, nation, and nations of the world.

For more information visit: www.theprayerfurnace.org
www.facebook.com/theprayerfurnace
Or contact us at: info@theprayerfurnace.org
540.834.2340

MAPS
PRAY | TRAIN | SEND

Do you feel a calling to go to the nations? Is traveling around the world with the Gospel something that has interested you? Consider the Missions and Prayer School (MAPS).

MAPS is a 3-Phase training program in Fredericksburg, VA, designed to equip young leaders for the unique dynamics of prayer and missions in this generation. Each of the 3 phases will have a particular focus as well as a missional assignments incorporated into it. This is a full-time and residential ministry school.

There is a Phase 1 "Immersion" option for those who want to take a semester to dive into prayer and missions but aren't quite sure yet whether they desire to or should devote the next few years to that specific kind of training.

For more information visit: www.themapschool.com
www.facebook.com/themapschool
Or contact us at: info@themapschool.com
540.834.2340